THE
SHADOW OF
SCOTUS

*Philosophy and Faith
in Pre-Reformation Scotland*

Alexander Broadie

T&T CLARK
EDINBURGH

T&T CLARK LTD
59 GEORGE STREET
EDINBURGH EH2 2LQ
SCOTLAND

First published 1995

ISBN 0 567 09734 X HB
ISBN 0 567 29295 9 PB

1001260028

British Library Cataloguing-in-Publication Data
A catalogue record for this book is available from the British Library

Typeset by Waverley Typesetters, Galashiels
Printed and bound in Great Britain by Bookcraft Ltd, Avon

Contents

Contents

Preface

THIS BOOK is a lightly edited version of a set of six Gifford lectures delivered at the University of Aberdeen in Spring 1994 as part of the University's quincentenary celebration. A Gifford lecturer undertakes a formidable task, that of 'promoting, advancing, and diffusing the study of natural theology' – a phrase employed by Lord Gifford in the Will establishing the lectures that bear his name. Since Lord Gifford goes on to state that true knowledge of God, knowledge such as is afforded by natural theology, is 'the means of man's highest well being, and the security of his upward progress', it is plain that he had in mind a subject of the greatest conceivable importance to humankind.

He lists in his Will the topics he regards as coming under the heading of 'natural theology'. Among them is that of the relations which people bear to God. But a person can stand in many relations to God, some of these of greater significance for natural theology and some of less. One of particular significance is the relation in which a person of faith is bound to God considered as the object of that faith. It is upon the concept of faith that the following six lectures are focused. Since the philosophers and theologians whose ideas on faith are discussed here are from Pre-Reformation Scotland, and since, especially, the final two lectures are devoted to a study of the ideas of John Mair and his associates, who lived in Scotland in the late-fifteenth and early-sixteenth centuries, my discussion will indicate some of the philosophical and theological ideas current in the Scottish universities at the time of the founding of King's College, Aberdeen. And in this context it is helpful to remember that Hector Boece, friend and colleague of John Mair, was the first principal of the College.

My colleague, Dr C. F. J. Martin, helped me, in the course of numerous conversations, to understand Duns Scotus's arguments better. Miss P. S. Martin made many suggestions, to the benefit of the text, on matters of style. I am glad of this opportunity to thank both for their help. Each of the lectures at Aberdeen was followed by lengthy and lively discussion. I benefited greatly from the exchanges, particularly the many that I had with Professor J. R. Cameron, to whom I owe a special debt of gratitude.

Unless otherwise stated the translations from Latin are my own.

A. B.
Glasgow 1995

Lecture 1

Faith as the space of philosophy: Duns Scotus to John Mair

RELIGIOUS FAITH is one species of faith amongst others, and perhaps not all people have it. But considered in its generic aspect faith permeates the lives of all of us, and there are therefore many different possible perspectives upon it. Here I shall view it from the perspective of mental philosophy. That there should be such a perspective on faith is suggested by the fact that giving one's assent, saying 'yes', as an act of faith is a mental act, and the question therefore arises as to which mental powers are involved whenever such an act is performed. That question can appropriately be addressed to mental philosophy.

Most philosophers carry with them into their enquiries knowledge of the contributions that their predecessors have made to the philosophical questions of perennial concern. Since the occasion for these lectures is the quincentenary of King's College, Aberdeen, the writings that I shall carry most explicitly into this enquiry into faith are those of philosophers and theologians from Pre-Reformation Scotland, especially thinkers who lived around the time of the founding of King's College. Consequently these lectures will present a picture of the kinds of philosophical and theological discussions that were familiar to the students who attended the University of Aberdeen during the first years of its existence.

But who are these early Scottish philosophers? The name of one of them, John Duns Scotus (c. 1266–1308),[1] to whom I shall be devoting most attention in lectures two and three, is familiar to everyone; in 1993 he was accorded the title *Beatus* – Blessed. It was not only in virtue of the quality of his philosophy that the decision to beatify him was taken, but all the same the philosophy was an essential part of the man beatified. I believe him to be Scotland's greatest philosopher, yet, as I have indicated, there are also other philosophers from Pre-

Reformation Scotland, and very few know of their existence. I am speaking here of one of the best-kept secrets of Scottish culture.

Scotus was not the first philosopher from this country. He had several predecessors, distinguished in their own day, whose writings have come down to us. One in particular whose existence we should at least note here is Richard Scot (c. 1123–73), who is usually referred to, with French pronunciation, as Richard de St Victor, though his Latin name, which tells us rather more and is rarely mentioned, is Ricardus de Sancto Victore Scotus.[2] Richard Scot of the Abbey of St Victor, Paris, studied under the Abbey's most famous theologian Hugh of St Victor, and in 1162 succeeded him as prior. Richard, who died less than half a century before the founding of the Order of Friars Minor, the Franciscans, had a great influence on the philosophical and theological stance with which that Order quickly came to be associated. Richard Scot placed love at the centre of his theological system because he believed love to be a central feature of the universe, in virtue both of God's love for the created world and also of the commandment that we love God with all our heart. On these matters Richard was a follower of St Anselm of Canterbury. A century after Richard, the Franciscan Duns Scotus, in his turn, followed Richard on these same matters.

Intermediate in time between Richard Scot and Duns Scotus was their compatriot Michael Scot (died c. 1236), who was an important link in the chain of transmission of Aristotle's works from the Muslim world, via Spain, to the Christian West. In addition, with the help of Spanish-Jewish colleagues Michael Scot made translations into Latin of Arabic commentaries, in particular those of Averroes, on Aristotle.[3] Though there is evidence that he worked for some time in Scotland, we lack proof that he engaged in any philosophical activity while here.

Certainly there were many scholars from Scotland, such as Richard Scot and Michael Scot, who studied and worked abroad. However, not all did. Scotland contained great religious houses, and no doubt philosophy was taught in them along with the theological instruction that was surely given. One thinker whose work has never received due attention is the twelfth-century abbot of Dryburgh, Adam Scot, many of whose writings are extant, even if not available in recent editions.[4] His theological works contain philosophical insights which may have been expounded in classes which he conducted in Dryburgh Abbey.

Richard Scot spent his working life in Paris, and Michael Scot spent much of his in Toledo, Bologna, and as astrologer to the court of

Frederick II of Sicily. Duns Scotus worked at the Universities of Oxford and Cambridge, Paris and Cologne. There is a question as to why so many of Scotland's earliest philosophers worked outside this country. A plausible explanation is simply that we did not at that time have any universities. Once the University of St Andrews was established, however, followed within the same century by the Universities of Glasgow and Aberdeen, the situation was transformed, and was transformed especially to the benefit of philosophy, though conventional wisdom would not have us believe this. I shall dwell on this last point.

All agree that poets made a priceless contribution to our literary canon during the century or so following the founding of Scotland's first university. The period is the age of the makars, the lowland poets, Robert Henryson, William Dunbar, Gavin Douglas, and others. In his *Lament for the Makaris* Dunbar names many poets whose works are now lost. But in any case the extant poetical writings of the period are of sufficient quantity and quality to stamp the age with a distinctive character.

Historical judgment on this matter has been very unfair. I do not mean in the least – how could I? – to be stinting about the magnificence, the magisterial presence, of the poetry of that age when I say that the overwhelming emphasis which has been placed on the poetical achieve-ments of the fifteenth- and early-sixteenth-century Scottish literary heritage promotes a distorted image of that heritage. I believe the poetical achievement to have been fully matched by the Scottish philosophers who were contemporaries of the poets, though the writings of the philosophers disappeared into near oblivion and are only now being rescued. It is not difficult to explain why the writings of the philosophers slipped out of sight, but explanations in terms of historical causation cannot ever amount to justification of the events thus explained. It was despite the quality of the writings, not because of their quality, that they ceased to be read.

Considerations of politeness dictate that I introduce the philosophers I have in mind, since the last three lectures will make extensive use of their writings. All of them were Catholic priests, a fact which assumes especial significance in relation to the question of why their writings ceased to be studied in Scotland after the Reformation. The same point also explains why the writings of one Scot in particular, John Mair, continued to be listed as required reading in the universities of Spain, which of course did not undergo a Protestant Reformation. He was quoted frequently by his pupil, the great Spanish philosopher Francisco

Vitoria, and also by Francisco Suarez, greatest philosopher-theologian of the Society of Jesus, an Order founded by Ignatius Loyola, who attended Mair's lectures at Paris.

That there was great liveliness on the Scottish scene at the time of the foundation of St Andrews University is shown by the fact that its first rector, Lawrence of Lindores (d. 1437), banned the teaching of the realist philosophy of Albert the Great, teacher of St Thomas Aquinas, and insisted that the philosophy courses should instead have a nominalist bias.[5] His action in issuing the ban suggests that, practically from the first day of our first university, the philosophers in Scotland were in heated dispute with each other. Nominalism, which I shall discuss in the next lecture, had a brief pre-eminence during Lawrence of Lindores' rectorship. But it is evident that there were a number, indeed a majority, of closet realists in the arts faculty, for in the year following Lawrence's death his ban was revoked.[6]

This early battle in St Andrews has symbolic significance in relation to the Scottish philosophical tradition. Though I shall not attempt it here, I think it is possible to demonstrate that that tradition is marked by a continuing dispute between nominalists and realists, and that therefore generations of Scottish philosophers after Lawrence of Lindores inherited a dispute that has been in the system from the start. In the period of the Enlightenment, for example, Thomas Reid's attack on Hume was essentially a realist attack on an extreme nominalism.[7]

It is therefore a matter of more than merely passing interest that John Ireland (c. 1440–95), a graduate of St Andrews and Scotland's most important philosopher of the latter part of the fifteenth century, was caught up in a royal ban on nominalist teaching. On leaving St Andrews, John Ireland matriculated at the University of Paris, rising to become its rector, briefly, in 1469. Five years later Louis XI issued an ordinance approving the teaching of realist philosophers – he names Aristotle, Aquinas and Duns Scotus – and prohibiting the teaching of nominalists, such as William Ockham. A deputation, of which John Ireland was a member, was sent to the king to argue for the revocation of the ban. However, the ban remained in force till 1481, by which time John Ireland was back in this country.[8] In 1490 he completed his *Mirror of Wisdom*, containing a number of passages of considerable theological interest relating to the concept of will. I shall deal with those passages in the fourth lecture.

John Ireland was one of a large number of Scots at the University of Paris. In the later 1470s that contingent was joined by James Liddell

(d. prob. after 1519) from Aberdeen.[9] He graduated with a master's degree in 1483, and in the following year began to teach at Paris. In 1495, the year of the founding of a university in his home town, he became the first-ever Scot to have a book of his printed in his own lifetime. Given my belief that the Scots are a nation of philosophers, I find it peculiarly appropriate that that first-ever book by a Scot printed in his own lifetime was a work on philosophy. Its title is *Conceptuum et signorum* – 'On concepts and signs', and there is a single extant copy, in the National Library of Scotland. The book is an investigation into the natural signs and conventional symbols by which we experience the world and communicate our experiences to others.[10] The book is sufficiently important in relation to the Scottish cultural tradition to merit a quincentenary celebration all to itself in Aberdeen, its author's home town.

The topic of Liddell's book was a popular one among Scottish philosophers, several of whom, in the generation after Liddell, wrote substantial treatises devoted entirely to matters dealt with in the *Conceptuum et signorum*. The authors of those treatises were all members of the circle of John Mair. Hugh MacDiarmid coined the slogan 'Back to Dunbar' as a rallying cry, hoping to persuade us to look back beyond Burns and the Enlightenment to the works of William Dunbar and the other poets of the Pre-Reformation period. In the light of work done recently on John Mair and his circle, and with MacDiarmid's slogan in mind, George Davie has coined the slogan 'Back to John Mair' as a rallying cry, hoping to persuade us to look back beyond Hume and the Enlightenment to the works of Mair and his colleagues.[11] Who then was Mair?

Born near Haddington c. 1467, he attended school in that town, the same school at which, a generation later, John Knox was a pupil.[12] Mair was a student at the University of Paris, rising to become Professor of Theology there. He quickly acquired a Europe-wide reputation as a teacher, theologian, philosopher and logician. He returned to Scotland in 1518 to take up the post of principal of the University of Glasgow, before transferring briefly to St Andrews. After a further short period in Paris, he returned to St Andrews c. 1531, duly became Provost of St Salvator's College at the University, and remained in that post till his death in 1550, aged about eighty-three. He was a colleague of Erasmus at Paris, and his lectures there were attended not only by Loyola and Vitoria as already mentioned, but also by Buchanan, Rabelais, Calvin and Vives. At St Andrews he was the theology tutor of John Knox, who was later to refer to Mair as 'an oracle on matters of religion'.[13] He also wrote more than forty books, all of them extant.[14] We are speaking therefore of a thinker pre-eminent in his day.

Among his colleagues at Paris were a number of Scots, some of whom returned to Scotland to take up major posts, in education, the Church and the law. These men were among the great teachers, preachers and pleaders of their age in Scotland. One is the Dundonian Hector Boece (c. 1465–1536), first principal of the University of Aberdeen, where he worked from c. 1497 till his death. His *Explicatio quorundam vocabulorum* is a wonderfully clear and incisive account of the science of logic.[15] He was an admirer of Mair, referring to him as 'a profound theologian, whose writings, like brightest torches, have shed a glorious light on the Christian religion'[16] – indeed the admiration was mutual – and it is probable that Mair was on Boece's reading lists when the latter lectured at Aberdeen. Others among the Scots at Paris during Mair's stay there were George Lokert of Ayr (c. 1485–1547), rector of St Andrews University and dean of Glasgow, Robert Galbraith (c. 1483–1544), senator of the College of Justice in Edinburgh and author of one of the great works of late-medieval logic, William Manderston (c. 1485–1552), graduate of Glasgow and rector of St Andrews University, Gilbert Crab of Aberdeen (c. 1482–1522), a prolific writer who published a commentary on Aristotle's *Politics* while yet an undergraduate, and David Cranston (c. 1479–1512), of the Glasgow diocese, Mair's favourite pupil, who died aged about thirty-three, a few weeks after being awarded a doctorate of theology by Paris. It is upon members of this distinguished circle of philosophers and theologians that I shall focus in my later lectures.[17]

These men could not ignore the commanding presence of Duns Scotus, who had lived two centuries earlier. Whether they agreed with him or disagreed, they were aware of him, not just as a great philosophical predecessor but as a Scot. Mair, for example, refers to him rather often not as Scotus, but simply as *conterraneus*[18] ('my fellow countryman'), and indeed in his *History of Greater Britain* Mair is happy to include the detail, not entirely relevant to the narrative, that Scotus was born just a few leagues from Mair's own birth place. Something of Mair's interest in and attitude to Scotus emerges in the following important passage from Mair's *History*:

> Near to him [sc. Richard Middleton] in date, only later, wrote John Duns, that subtle doctor, who was a Scottish Briton, for he was born at Duns, a village eight miles distant from England, and separated from my own home

by seven or eight leagues only. When he was no more than a boy, but had been grounded in grammar, he was taken by two Scottish Minorite friars to Oxford, for at that time there existed no university in Scotland. By the favour of those friars he lived in the convent of the Minorites at Oxford, and he made his profession in the religion of the Blessed Francis. As he was a man of the loftiest understanding and the keenest powers in debate, his designation of 'the subtle' was fully justified. At Oxford he made such progress that he left behind him for the admiration of after ages a monumental work the Metaphysics and the four books of the Sentences. These writings of his are commonly called the English or the Oxford work. When he was afterwards summoned by the Minorites of Paris to that city, he produced there another set of lectures on the Sentences, more compendious than the first edition, and at the same time more useful. These lectures we have but lately caused to be printed with metal types.[19] In the end he went to Cologne, and there died while still a young man.[20]

I believe that Scotus cast a long shadow across the Scottish philosophical scene, and I hope to make a start in these lectures on providing evidence for this claim.

At the beginning I nailed my colours to the mast by saying that I believed Duns Scotus to be Scotland's greatest philosopher. On the other hand there are many who have regarded him as merely a notable representative of the logic-chopping schoolmen, a desiccated pedlar of soulless wares. Nevertheless we should not lose sight of the fact that he inspired Gerard Manley Hopkins, a free-flying spirit if ever there was one, who found in Scotus a companion spirit, rejoiced in his ideas, and celebrated him in his sonnet 'Duns Scotus's Oxford':

> Yet ah! this air I gather and release
> He lived on; these weeds and waters, these walls are what
> He haunted who of all men most sways my spirits to peace;
>
> Of realty the rarest-veinèd unraveller; a not
> Rivalled insight, be rival Italy or Greece.

> (lines 9–13)

What was it that made Scotus the object of the intense intellectual passion of no less than Hopkins? Part of the answer is that Hopkins found that same intensity of intellectual passion in Scotus also, a philosopher who, as already stated, placed the concept of love at the centre of his system and who wrote with energy and fire when love was the reality he was dealing with – as it often was, for it was basic to his metaphysics, his mental philosophy, and his ethics.

7

In focusing thus upon love, Scotus reveals himself as a member of the Order of Friars Minor; his Franciscan background was of central importance in the development of his philosophy. No-one philosophises in a cultural vacuum, and, as is obvious, knowledge of the cultural context of a philosopher helps us to understand his philosophy; it can never hinder us. It is for this reason that I emphasise the fact that Scotus wrote not merely as a Christian, but as a Franciscan. His Order defined the character of his faith, and it was precisely upon love that that faith was focused. Faith was the space of Scotus's philosophy. It not only set the agenda for his philosophising but also explains the intensity of his writing.

A phrase especially associated with St Anselm of Canterbury applies with great force to Scotus. No brief passage has served more to give direction to Western philosophy than the 'ontological argument' occupying those few lines in Anselm's *Proslogion*. It had been Anselm's intention to name that work *Fides quaerens intellectum* – Faith seeking understanding. But though he eventually settled for the title *Proslogion* – Soliloquy, the earlier title was more revealing of the content not only of that short work but also of Anselm's entire philosophical and theological output. He was a man of faith. His faith had certain objects, most especially, God and God's knowledge, His impassibility, mercy and justice, and it was about these objects of his faith that Anselm philosophised because he wished to understand as fully as he was able the content of his faith.

Scotus's writings, no less than Anselm's, come under the heading 'Faith seeking understanding'. And something has to be said about this heading for it can puzzle, if not exasperate, modern secular philosophers. There is a certain view of philosophy as an activity whose direction is dictated by argument, and not at all by the prejudices, likes and dislikes, of the philosopher. In philosophy, reason, not emotion, is given its head. On this view, philosophy is not merely an exercise in *inventio*, the art of finding arguments which support positions already adopted on whatever grounds. A criticism often levelled at philosophers in the mould of Anselm and Scotus is precisely that they begin by knowing exactly what they believe, and employ philosophy as a handmaid to their religion to confer an aura of intellectual respectability on their religious *prejudgments*. I shall now seek to argue that this is not a good reason for dismissing philosophers such as Anselm and Scotus, whose philosophy grows within the space of their faith.

It might be pointed out that some exercises in *inventio*, the discovery of arguments in support of what is already judged true, are not thought to be intellectually disreputable. As one distinguished medievalist has remarked, Bertrand Russell, who accused medieval philosophers of using philosophy to prove what they already held true, himself devoted three hundred and sixty tightly argued pages to a proof that $1 + 1 = 2$ (*Principia Mathematica* *54.43). This was not a case of Russell following the argument whithersoever it might lead. He knew from the start exactly what his goal was. And in that case, surely Russell was ill-placed to criticise medieval philosophers for using philosophy in order to provide such rational basis as they could find for propositions which they in any case accepted.[21]

This is a nice *tu quoque* argument, but it is not, I believe, an appropriate way to respond to Russell's attack on medieval philosophy, for what Russell set out to prove was not simply that $1 + 1 = 2$, but that mathematics can be generated from logic. Russell's work therefore was not an exercise in finding a proof for what was in any case known, but in finding a proof for a claim that he had previously regarded as no more than a matter of speculation. I should prefer therefore to respond in a different way to the argument that since medieval philosophers use their philosophy to try to prove what they already believe, their philosophy is somehow flawed and should be dismissed.

We need to take seriously the formula 'faith seeking understanding'. It is untrue that at the start of their philosophising the medieval philosophers already knew exactly what they believed. We find them again and again asking themselves: 'But *what* do I believe?' They are not asking what the religious formulae are to which they, as members of their faith community, have to give assent. They know the formulae perfectly well. What they want to know is what those formulae mean. So, as *fideles*, people of faith, and as philosophers, they go in search of understanding.

For example, it is, I believe, preferable to interpret the so-called 'ontological argument' of St Anselm's *Proslogion*, not as a demonstration of the existence of God, but instead as a systematic investigation into God's mode of existence. As *fidelis quaerens intellectum* St Anselm was not seeking proof of God's existence, but he was seeking to understand His existence, and it was through his philosophising that he came to do so. If this is a correct interpretation, then the question he addressed was not *whether* God exists but *how* He does.

Admittedly Anselm tells us near the start of the Preface to the *Proslogion*: 'I began to ask myself whether perhaps it might be possible to find a single argument that for its proof required no other than itself, and that by itself would suffice to prove that God truly exists [*quia deus vere est*]'.[22] Furthermore, the heading that Anselm provides for the first of the crucial two chapters is: 'That God truly exists' – '*Quod vere sit Deus*'. These two passages do indeed appear to imply that he is about to present a proof of God's existence. But the matter is not so straightforward. Why does Anselm say in the Preface that his project is to prove that God *truly* exists and why is the title to Chapter Two: 'That God *truly* exists'? What contribution does the word 'truly' – '*vere*' make? Why is the title of the chapter not simply: 'That God exists' – '*Quod sit Deus*'? To answer this, we have to consider what it is with which *true* existence should be contrasted. And it can be demonstrated that Anselm does have a contrast in mind. In the *Monologion*, written one year before the *Proslogion*, Anselm speaks about us creatures in the following terms: 'Since that which [creatures] were does not now exist, and that which they will be does not yet exist, and that which they are in the fleeting, knife-edged, and scarcely existent present scarcely exists, since, therefore, they are as mutable as this they are rightly said not to have simple, perfect and absolute existence, and are said almost not to exist and scarcely to exist.'[23] To exist as we do is to exist but only just; to do so any less would be not to exist at all. To use Anselm's word to describe our status, we *scarcely* exist.

The contrast with God in whom Anselm has faith could not be greater. It is God's nature to exist, and His non-existence is therefore impossible. To exist without the possibility of not doing so is to exist *truly*. And when Anselm heads his chapter: 'That God *truly* exists', he is signalling that he will demonstrate that God's existence is unlike that of creatures. That something can exist more or less truly is plainly indicated when Anselm writes: 'You alone, then, of all things most truly exist and therefore of all things possess existence to the highest degree; for anything else does not exist as truly, and so possesses existence to a lesser degree.'[24] Anselm is about to undertake an investigation into the nature of divine existence, the conclusion of which will be that God's existence is such that it is impossible for Him not to exist.[25] Anselm therefore starts from a faith which constitutes the space of his philosophy, and wins his way through to a depth of understanding of the nature of the divine existence that he had not previously reached.

This is a far cry from the interpretation of Anselm's *Proslogion* according to which he starts by having faith that God exists and then proceeds to prove that the God in whom he has faith does in fact exist. The task he sets himself is more interesting than that. We should recall here words Anselm penned as a preliminary to his so-called ontological argument: '[Your servant] yearns to see you, and your countenance is too far from him. He desires to come close to you, and your dwelling place is inaccessible. He longs to find you, and he does not know where you are. He is eager to seek you out, and he does not know your countenance. Lord, you are my God and my Lord, and I have never seen you.'[26] These are not the words of a man about to present a proof of God's existence. They are the words of a man who is as sure of God's existence as he is of his own, but who seeks understanding of that existence, seeks to 'know God's countenance'. The phrase '*fides quaerens intellectum*' encapsulates this position perfectly.

It can be demonstrated that much of Duns Scotus's philosophy is related in that same way to his faith. That is, he does not use philosophy to prove what he already knows, or use it to convince others of the intellectual respectability of something to which they could otherwise hardly be expected to give serious attention. Instead he uses philosophy to clarify the objects of his faith, so that something seen through a glass darkly comes to be seen with clarity. In this sense, for Scotus no less than for Anselm, faith is the space of philosophy.

Yet the act of faith itself which is directed to those obscure objects also stands in need of philosophical investigation for, as stated at the start, if saying 'yes' as an act of faith is a mental act, a philosophical question arises as to which mental powers are involved in its production. There are two obvious candidates, intellect and will. As regards intellect, to give assent to a proposition, whether doing so as an act of faith or otherwise, is to make a judgment; it is to judge that a given proposition is true, and there is a long-held and widely held view that the intellect is the faculty by which we judge.

It might be maintained, in addition, that acceptance of a proposition on faith involves at least a judgment that the proposition is not contradictory, and may therefore be accepted without contravening the laws of logic; for to assent to a proposition, whether as an act of faith or not, is, as just said, to judge it to be true, and a proposition cannot without contradiction be judged both contradictory and true. But judging of the contradictoriness or otherwise of a proposition is an

11

act of intellect. An assent of faith therefore cannot be given without the intellect being engaged.

I am hesitant about this further argument, however, in view of the thinking that lies behind the famous phrase associated with Tertullian: '*Credo quia absurdum*' – 'I believe because it is absurd'. Tertullian did write: 'The son of God died. It is by all means to be believed because it is absurd [*ineptum*]. And he was buried and rose again. The fact is certain because it is impossible.'[27] Perhaps *ineptum* should in this context be translated 'absurd' – there is room for dispute about that. Nevertheless whether or not Tertullian said *Credo quia absurdum*, the phrase does represent a strand of Christian theologising, and may indeed encompass in the minds of some (even if not in the mind of Tertullian) the conviction that the perceived contradictoriness of a proposition should not by itself be a bar to the *fidelis* assenting to it. I should say at once, however, that members of John Mair's circle would reject out of hand as itself absurd the idea that a proposition perceived to be contradictory could be an appropriate object of an assent of faith. More of that later.

As regards will, there is a common view that accepting a proposition on faith is something over which we have control; it is something that we can decide to do. Somebody tells me something. I do not have to, I am not compelled to, take his word for truth. But all the same I decide to give my firm assent to what he has said. Such a response, which is a familiar if not an everyday occurrence, involves in an unspectacular way a leap of faith. All the philosophers with whom I shall be dealing held that assents of faith involve essentially such exercises of will, where will is contrasted with natural necessity – a contrast which I shall examine later when discussing Scotus's theory of freedom.

I have now given at least two reasons for taking seriously the hypothesis that faith is a product of intellect and will, and in due course I shall provide further arguments for this position. My conclusion will be that it is a product of the two mental powers jointly but of neither separately. That conclusion will of course prompt enquiry, which will duly be made, into the precise role that intellect and will each play in the production of faith.

If an act of will is a partial cause of faith, and if will is the faculty through which we act freely, and therefore in a manner undetermined by natural causation, then an assent of faith is a free act, by which I mean to imply that in the moment in which we give such an assent we could equally in those very same circumstances refuse to give it. This conclusion has large pastoral implications, for if the giving of an assent of faith is a free act, it follows that it, and the opposite act of refusing to give such an assent, can justifiably draw upon the agent praise or blame, as with all his free acts, and it can draw upon him also whatever recompense is commensurate with the praise and with the blame. The Church can therefore regard itself as entitled to consider how it should treat those who refuse to accept the Good Word when it is presented plainly to them, or worse, who reject it after having previously accepted it. We read in the Gospel that we are commanded to believe, and we are told there that those who do not believe will be condemned – *Qui vero non crediderit condemnabitur* (Mark 16.16). This verse[28] is read most easily as based upon the doctrine that an assent of faith is a free act. I shall explore this matter in detail in connection with John Mair's treatment of the issue.

I said earlier that faith permeates the lives of all of us. I wish to return to this claim and to acknowledge that some may disagree with, even bridle at it. They may say to the contrary that they have never been persons of faith or perhaps that they have lost their faith and find that they can get along quite nicely, perhaps much better, without it, and that certainly their lives are not permeated with it. I must therefore undertake to justify my claim that the lives of all of us are indeed permeated with faith.

A great deal of what we know is accepted by us on the authority of others. Though we have not ourselves witnessed a given event, someone else tells us that he has, tells us what he saw, and we take his word for it. This way of acquiring knowledge is so routine a part of our lives that, as with knowledge acquired by sense perception, we hardly notice that the process is taking place. The knowledge we acquire through sense perception forms a significant proportion of the total knowledge that we each possess, and philosophers have had a great deal to say about it. But what we acquire from infancy onwards by accepting the authority of others also forms a significant proportion of our total knowledge. Without that acceptance of authority our knowledge, such as it might be, would not be recognisably human. Yet the authority of others is a medium for the acquisition of knowledge, to which philosophers have on the whole paid rather slight attention. We listen to people, and we read; and make what we hear and read part of ourselves, adding it to the vast reservoir of knowledge which we bring to bear whenever we, as spectators, look out upon the world and, as agents, seek to interact with it. Through our routine acceptance of authority we witness, though vicariously, countless events, and acquire also principles of action and explanation, through which we become fitted for human society.

A central feature of our stance towards others is our disposition to credit people with honesty. Modern economies are run on credit, but our entire culture is based on credit in a sense of that word that goes far beyond the merely economic. We put our faith in people. Someone might let us down of course but could do so only because we began by putting our faith in him. And even when we have become untrusting, this does not mean that we no longer put our faith in anyone. It is not just that we cannot do that and remain in human society. It is that we cannot help having faith. We continue to have faith in most people while we distrust a very few.

Yet the term 'faith' has acquired a much narrower usage. We can have faith in many sorts of things, and yet when someone is described as a person of faith, or it is said of him that he has lost his faith, we will assume that it is religious faith that is meant. In this sense we speak of the great faiths of the world. We do not include among them the faith an infant has in his or her parents, or the faith that spouses have in each other, though these are certainly faiths of sorts and have countless millions of adherents. We mean instead Judaism, Christianity, Islam, and so on. But faith, meaning religious faith, is generically the same as the faith that we place in our friends, in our neighbours, and indeed in people in general. Religious faith is distinctive, not in respect of what makes it faith but in respect of its object, that is, in respect of what makes the faith religious.

The significance of this point lies in the fact that a good deal of philosophy can be written about faith without attention being paid at all to the specifically religious variety. John Mair and his colleagues were well aware – as how could they not be? – of the fact that the concept of faith covers phenomena other than religious faith, and I shall be exploring their discussions of the concept of faith in the generic sense of that term. It is with that sense in mind that I say that faith permeates the lives of all of us. I think that those who would bridle at this claim would do so because they interpret me as being so wrong, and perhaps also as being so presumptuous, as to ascribe religious faith to them.

I began by saying that I shall be dealing with faith from the perspective of mental philosophy, paying particular attention to the question of the relation between faith on the one hand and the mental powers of intellect and will on the other. In the next lecture I shall make a start on this project by investigating those two mental powers. John Duns Scotus, *Doctor Subtilis* to his medieval successors, and now *Beatus*, will be my guide.

NOTES

1. For a general introduction to his work see F. Copleston, *A History of Philosophy*, vol. 2, pt. 2, pp. 199–274. See also Allan B. Wolter, O.F.M., 'Duns Scotus, John', in Paul Edwards (ed.), *The Encyclopedia of Philosophy*, vol. 2, pp. 427–36, and *Duns Scotus on the Will and Morality*, Selected and translated with an Introduction by Allan B. Wolter, O.F.M., Introduction, for an insightful survey of his philosophical system. There is no critical edition of the complete works of Scotus. One is planned by the Scotistic Commission. The first volume appeared in 1950.
2. His writings are collected in J.-P. Migne, *Patrologia Latina*, vol. 196. There is a modern edition of his most important work *De Trinitate*, ed. J. Ribailler, in *Textes Philosophiques du Moyen Age*, 6. This includes bio-bibliographical details. See also the brief but helpful translation of parts of the *De Trinitate* in J. F. Wippel and A. B. Wolter, O.F.M., *Medieval Philosophy: From St Augustine to Nicholas of Cusa*, pp. 210–26.
3. For an account of his life and work see Lynn Thorndyke, *Michael Scot*. For his role in the transmission of Aristotle see N. Kretzmann, A. Kenny, J. Pinborg (eds), *The Cambridge History of Later Medieval Philosophy*, pp. 48–52, 58–9.
4. For details of his life and work see James Bulloch, *Adam of Dryburgh*. His works are in *Patrologia Latina*, vol. 153, cols. 799–884; vol. 184, cols. 869–80; vol. 198, cols. 91–872.
5. Annie I. Dunlop, *Acta Facultatis Artium Universitatis Sancti Andree 1413–1588*. See entry for 16 February 1418.
6. Ibid., entry for 14 November 1438.
7. A. Broadie, *The Tradition of Scottish Philosophy*, chs. 8–9.
8. For biographical and other details see J. H. Burns, 'John Ireland and "The Meroure of Wyssdome"', *Innes Review*, vol. 6, 1955, pp. 77–98; Brother Bonaventure, 'The popular theology of John Ireland', *Innes Review*, vol. 13, 1962, pp. 130–46; J. H. Burns, 'John Ireland: Theology and public affairs in the late fifteenth century', *Innes Review*, vol. 41, 1990, pp. 151–81; F. Quinn (ed.), *The Meroure of Wyssdome by Johannes de Irlandia*, vol. II, Introduction; C. McDonald, *The Meroure of Wyssdome by Johannes de Irlandia*, vol. III, Introduction.
9. See W. Beattie, 'Two notes on fifteenth century printing: I. Jacobus Ledelh', *Edinburgh Bibliographical Society Transactions*, vol. 3, 1950, pp. 75–7.

10. For detailed exposition of its contents see A. Broadie, 'James Liddell on concepts and signs' in M. Lynch, A. A. Macdonald, I. Cowan (eds), *The Renaissance in Scotland*, pp. 82–94.

11. G. E. Davie, *The Crisis of the Democratic Intellect*.

12. For brief biography of Mair see A. Broadie, *George Lokert: Late-Scholastic Logician*, ch. 1.

13. W. C. Dickinson (ed.), *John Knox's History of the Reformation in Scotland*, vol. 1, p. 15.

14. See J. Durkan, 'The school of John Major: Bibliography', *Innes Review*, vol. 1, pp. 140–57; also J. K. Farge, *Biographical Register of Paris Doctors of Theology 1500–1536*, pp. 304–11.

15. Sole extant copy is in Glasgow University Library.

16. Hector Boece, *Murthlacensium et Aberdonensium Episcoporum Vitae*, ed. and tr. J. Moir, p. 89.

17. For a detailed discussion of the logic of these men see A. Broadie, *The Circle of John Mair: Logic and Logicians in Pre-Reformation Scotland*.

18. For example: 'Sed pro modo conterranei notabis – but after the fashion of my compatriot you will note . . .', Mair, *In Secundum Sententiarum* 1vb; 'Maxima conterranei intelligitur in agente naturali solum' – 'the maxim of my compatriot should be understood to apply only to a natural agent', *ibid*. 59ra–rb; '. . . non pono distinctionem realem vel formalem more conterranei inter voluntatem et intellectum' – '. . . I do not posit a real or a formal distinction between will and intellect in the manner of my fellow countryman', *ibid*. 96vb; 'Conterraneus vero ponit haecceitatem esse principium individuationis' – 'My compatriot lays it down indeed that haecceity is the principle of individuation', Mair, *In Quartum Sententiarum* 330vb; '*In Primum Sententiarum* conterranei mei Ioannis Duns' – 'The Commentary on Book One of the *Sentences* by my compatriot John Duns', Dedicatory Epistle to Mair's *In Primum Sententiarum*.

19. The other two men in the three-man team headed by Mair which edited the Paris edition of the *Sentences* (the *Reportata Parisiensia*) were the Franciscan James Rufin and Brother Peter de Sault. For valuable discussion of Mair's *History*, see Roger A. Mason, 'Kingship, nobility and Anglo-Scottish Union: John Mair's *History of Greater Britain* (1521)', *Innes Review*, vol. 41, 1990, pp. 182–222.

20. John Mair, *A History of Greater Britain as well England as Scotland*, pp. 206–7.

21. This argument is presented by A. Kenny in his Introduction to A. Kenny (ed.), *Aquinas: A Collection of Critical Essays*, p. 2.

22. 'Coepi mecum quaerere, si forte posset inveniri unum argumentum, quod nullo alio ad se probandum quam se solo indigeret, et solum ad astruendum quia deus vere est.' *Proslogion*, Preface; in *S. Anselmi . . . Opera Omnia*, ed. F. S. Schmitt, O.S.B., vol. 1, p. 93, lines 5–7.

23. 'Quoniam hoc quia fuerunt iam non est, illud autem scilicet quia erunt nondum est, et hoc quod in labili brevissimoque et vix existente praesenti sunt vix est; quoniam ergo tam mutabiliter sunt: non immerito negantur simpliciter et perfecte et absolute esse, et asseruntur fere non esse et vix esse.' *Monologion*, ch. 28; in *S. Anselmi . . . Opera Omnia*, p. 46, lines 12–16.

24. 'Solus igitur verissime omnium, et ideo maxime omnium habes esse: quia quidquid aliud est non sic vere, et idcirco minus habet esse.' In *Proslogion*, ch. 3; in *S. Anselmi . . . Opera Omnia*, p. 103, lines 7–9.

25. In my interpretation of St Anselm I have been particularly influenced by Karl Barth, especially his *Fides Quaerens Intellectum*, and by Anselm Stolz, especially his 'Anselm's theology in the Proslogion', tr. printed in J. Hick and A. C. McGill, *The Many-Faced Argument*, pp. 183–206.

26. 'Anhelat videre te, et nimis abest illi facies tua. Accedere ad te desiderat, et inaccessibilis est habitatio tua. Invenire te cupit, et nescit locum tuum. Quaerere te affectat, et ignorat vultum tuum. Domine, deus meus es, et dominus meus es, et numquam te vidi.' *Proslogion*, ch. 1; in *S. Anselmi . . . Opera Omnia*, p. 98, lines 9–13.

27. 'Et mortuus est dei filius: prorsus credibile est, quia ineptum est. Et sepultus resurrexit: certum est, quia impossibile.' In *Tertullian's Treatise on the Incarnation*, ed. and tr. Ernest Evans, p. 18, lines 24–6.

28. The authenticity of this verse is a matter of dispute. Chapter 16 from verse 9 to the end is almost certainly a late interpolation. Nevertheless the passage occurs in the Vulgate, and on that basis was treated as authentic by medieval theologians.

Lecture 2

Scotus, freedom and the power of intellect

IN THE first lecture I dwelt on St Anselm's formula '*fides quaerens intellectum*' – 'faith seeking understanding', and maintained that that formula describes the entire medieval philosophical enterprise. For during the Middle Ages faith set the agenda for philosophy, whose chief task was conceived to be the clarification of the objects of faith. In that sense the *Proslogion*, though very short, is a paradigm, perhaps even *the* paradigm, of medieval philosophy.

However, it is not only the objects of faith that call for philosophical investigation; so also does the concept of faith itself. With the exception of hell, a topic long overdue for theological rehabilitation, I shall not have a great deal to say about objects of faith. Instead the focus will be on the act of assenting in faith. Saying 'yes' as an act of faith is just one species of assent. Other sorts of act also fall under the genus 'assent', and since we learn a great deal about a thing by noting what it is that distinguishes it specifically from other things which are generically the same, I shall enquire into the nature of other sorts of assent, such as on the one hand the assent of mere opinion, and on the other hand the assent which we give to an evident perceptual truth, such as that this sheet of paper is white. But granted that assents of opinion, of faith and of knowledge are acts of three different sorts, what precisely is the difference between them? Members of the circle of John Mair had a good deal to say in reply to this question, and I shall be exploring their responses.

To anticipate subsequent discussion I should say now that the two notions that were given most work to do in the effort to differentiate the various forms of assent were those of will and intellect. In this lecture and the next, therefore, my attention will be directed to the analysis of these two faculties of mind. No Pre-Reformation Scottish philosopher looked more deeply than did Duns Scotus into the concepts of will and intellect, and his writings in this field exercised a profound influence on his Pre-Reformation Scottish successors. For these reasons it is to his writings that I shall now turn. The positions we establish concerning will and intellect will then be put to use in the later lectures as we come to grips with those late-medieval Scottish discussions on the nature of the assent of faith. More immediately I shall examine the faculties of will and intellect and the companion doctrines of voluntarism and intellectualism, and that examination will underpin the next lecture when I investigate the claim that it is will, and not intellect, that has primacy in the human mind.[1]

Voluntarists and intellectualists are in dispute with each other on a wide range of matters, with voluntarists emphasising the role of will and of our freedom in our relations with the world, in contradistinction to the intellectualists who emphasise the role of intellect and of our theoretical knowledge. The dispute is clearly articulated in the diverse responses to the question whether it is will or intellect that has primacy. Voluntarists say will has primacy and intellectualists ascribe primacy to intellect. I shall deal with this matter later.

First, I shall consider the opposition between voluntarists and intellectualists in respect of their teachings on the existential status of values. The crucial question in this area is whether values exist by an act of will or whether they are independent of will though available for inspection by our intellect. This is a particularly important question in the context of these lectures because an exaggerated version of Scotus's answer to this question is a major element in Scotism, as we shall see.

The dispute regarding values is best understood, I believe, if placed in the broader context of the dispute between nominalists and realists, the principal dispute in the universities of the Middle Ages. I stated in Lecture One that the tradition of Scottish philosophy is essentially the history of a dispute between nominalists and realists. The dispute between voluntarists and intellectualists is another major feature of that same tradition. The link between the disputes is that voluntarists tend to embrace nominalism and intellectualists realism. These terms are slogans at the moment, but I hope I shall have given them intellectual substance before this series of lectures is completed. The technical terms that I have just been casting round me were certainly not mere slogans for the men of the Middle Ages about whom I am speaking, for the issues for which the terms are shorthand closely concern matters of faith, and therefore concern the salvation of souls. Mistakes in this area were seen as dangerous. Of false teachings it could be said: *non solum mortua sunt sed mortifera* – not just dead but deadly.

In Lecture One I commented on the significance of the fact that Lawrence of Lindores, first rector of the University of St Andrews, banned the teaching of the realist philosophy of Albert the Great, a ban revoked as soon as Lawrence ceased to be rector, and we saw also that half a century later John Ireland was involved in a fight conducted by the University of Paris to overturn a ban imposed by Louis XI on the teaching of nominalist philosophy. Nominalism plainly touched a raw nerve in some people, and realism did likewise in others. One of the questions at issue was precisely whether values are objects of will, that is, are willed into existence, or whether they exist independent of will.

The fact that there are moral values prompts enquiry into the way they exist. One solution, sometimes called the 'divine command theory', focuses upon the role of God's will. It states that whether a mode of action is good or not depends upon God's will, as that will is expressed in His commands. On this account God is not constrained to command us to perform particular kinds of acts because He has an intellectual grasp of their goodness, but on the contrary His commanding us to perform them is itself what makes such acts good. In short, it is not through their being good that He comes to see them as good; it is that through His commanding them they become good. The goodness of such an act exists therefore by divine fiat. It is held in existence by an act of divine will.

One consequence thought by some to follow from this position is that it would be impossible for us to work out by an exercise of reason how we ought to behave. We must consult not reason but the divine will, howsoever that is made manifest. The doctrine that moral values are a consequence of the promulgation of the Commandments, the 'divine command theory', is thus thought to lead to ethical irrationalism; 'irrationalism' because according to this doctrine there is no rational basis to morality; the basis is divine command. It is commonly held that this form of irrationalism was taught by Scotus, and the doctrine is itself a central plank in the platform called Scotism. In Lecture Three, however, I shall demonstrate that Scotus taught a variety of ethical rationalism.

I do not know how many philosophers there are today, perhaps few, who would espouse the divine command theory of morality. But a secular version of the theistic theory has found favour in recent decades with very many philosophers. The modern secular version is to the effect that it is we human beings who create our values by an act of choice; and that, contrary to appearances, we are not merely confronted by our values, as if they had a totally distinct reality, existing independently of our will, and constraining us from the outside. This secular version of the divine command theory is to be found in certain of the writings of Sartre, and it is even on the title page of John L. Mackie's book on moral philosophy: *Ethics: Inventing Right and Wrong*.

Let us suppose that it is by an act of will, whether divine or creaturely, that the values by which we are to live are created, and suppose further that the will by which the values come into existence is not itself constrained by an intellectual act by which it is seen that those are the values which ought to be imposed. One conclusion is that the ethical theory here described is relativist. The moral law is relative to the will which produces it. A different will is free to produce a different set of moral values, and furthermore the same will, even and perhaps especially the divine will, can first will one set and then replace it by another.

I should say, as an aside and perhaps tendentiously, that the fact that voluntarism is a progenitor of ethical relativism might well, all by itself, make us hesitate to ascribe at any rate an unqualified voluntarism to Duns Scotus. Had the relevant Vatican authorities sensed the slightest whiff of relativism in Scotus's writings, he would assuredly not have been accorded the title *beatus*. The recent encyclical letter *Veritatis Splendor* by John Paul II contains a strongly worded denunciation of moral relativism in all its forms. For example, in its opening paragraph the encyclical describes the results of original sin in these terms: 'Giving himself over to relativism and scepticism man goes off in search of an illusory freedom apart from truth itself.' And later the encyclical declares: 'The primordial moral requirement of loving and respecting the person as an end and never as a mere means also implies, by its nature, respect for certain fundamental goods, without which one would fall into relativism and arbitrariness' (para. 48).

The presence of these and similar assertions in the encyclical is not however one of my reasons for thinking that Scotus was not in any full-blooded sense a relativist in his teaching on the existence of values. Their presence is merely a reason for holding that others who would speak with authority on the question of whether Scotus was a relativist or not must have thought that he was not one. My own reasons for holding that Scotus was no relativist are not grounded in the authority of others. Instead they are all firmly grounded in Scotus's own clear statements of his position – I am speaking about statements in which he attaches morality very firmly indeed to right reason, and makes clear his belief that we can by the exercise of reason learn how we ought to behave. Consulting the Bible is therefore not the only route to the truth about moral matters. We can of course consult the Bible, and will find the truth if we do. The point is that we can also find the truth by consulting our reason. In Lecture Three I shall cite some of the relevant passages in Scotus's *Ordinatio*.

I said earlier that voluntarists tend to embrace nominalism, and I should like now to begin to explore this link. Nominalists ascribe to the mind a role in the production of certain elements and features of our world that we naturally tend to think of as possessing an independent reality, that is, a reality independent of the activity of our mind. The adversaries of nominalists are realists, who say that those elements and features that we naturally think of as possessing an independent reality do in fact have such a reality. What elements and features? Among those in dispute between the two philosophical camps are, precisely, values. It follows from my characterisation of voluntarists that they will be nominalist about values, as I shall now explain.

Voluntarists hold that though our values appear to us to have an independent reality, they are in fact brought into existence, and maintained in existence, by an act of a mental power, a will. It does appear to us that we are confronted by our values which present themselves as distinct realities, existing independently of our will and constraining us from outside. But the nominalist invites us to note the word 'appear' in that description. That may be how values appear to us. But according to nominalists it is not how values do in fact exist. We are not always conscious of our mental acts by which we produce the things that we then see as independent. We have an almost magical ability to create things and then project them into the outer world so that they present themselves to us as if they are really of and from that outer world and not from us at all.

The nominalism about values that I have just described should be contrasted with realism about values. A value realist holds that values have an independent existence in the sense that the value possessed by a thing is not a matter subject to will. Nevertheless the value realist does hold that values are possible objects of intellect, available, that is to say, for discovery by intellect, and for inspection by it, leading to a judgment of the value's fittingness as a practical principle. This is an intellectualist view of values. Hence value realists are intellectualist and not voluntarist as regards their teaching on the mode of existence of values. And to the extent that the ethical realist holds that values are not objects of will, he rejects the doctrine of ethical relativism.

The dispute between realists and nominalists in the Middle Ages is commonly regarded as having been fought most especially in connection with the so-called problem of universals. I should therefore pause here to note that the dispute between voluntarists and intellectualists, those who emphasise the role of will, and those who emphasise the role of intellect, carried over into discussions of universals. Indeed there is a remarkable parallel between discussions about values and about universals, as we shall now see. I press this point here because Scotus has been regarded as the arch-voluntarist, and it is therefore as well to be clear about the kinds of thing that mark out the voluntarist's position.

Universals are the natures which are common to members of a given species by virtue of which they are members of their species. What is the mode of existence of these universals or common natures? Voluntarists hold characteristically that they are mental entities, the concepts formed in and by our intellect enabling us to classify the contents of our world. Otherwise stated, they are principles of classification. How we classify things is of course often a matter of choice, in the dual sense that, first, we construct principles of classification by choice, and secondly, it is commonly a matter of choice which principles of classification we bring to bear. That these concepts, which are principles of classification, are universal means simply that the concepts are predicable of an indefinitely large number of things. In so far as universals are concepts of the kind I have just been speaking about, universals certainly do not have an existence independently of us human beings. That is, the voluntarist tends to be nominalist on the subject of universals.

On the other hand the realist holds that universals have a relatively independent existence, being able to get along without our mental acts, so that for example, the sheephood in virtue of which particular animals are in the species sheep, cannot just be a concept in the mind, a principle of classification; on the contrary, sheephood must be in each and every sheep. And it is only in virtue of that common nature being in each of those animals that we are able to classify them the way we do. There is undoubtedly a great deal to be said in support of this realist position. The immediate point however upon which I wish to focus is that in so far as common natures exist as independent realities in things in the outer world, universals are indeed possible objects of intellect, though not objects of our will. Hence the realist is intellectualist about universals; he is not voluntarist about them.

In brief, the debate between voluntarists and intellectualists, between those who assign primacy to will and those who assign it to intellect, comes very close at times to being the debate between nominalists and realists, and, as already indicated, that latter debate has characterised the Western philosophical enterprise, and assuredly has characterised the Scottish philosophical tradition, from the start. Indeed it is still with us. I conclude that the dispute between voluntarists and intellectualists is of the first importance in the history of philosophy. It is easy to attach personal names to the dispute. As far as reputation goes, the great intellectualist is St Thomas Aquinas, and the great voluntarist is John Duns Scotus. Later I shall argue against this way of personalising the dispute, for it is easy, rather too easy, to exaggerate the philosophical distance between these two great thinkers.

There is a spectrum here, with extreme positions and intermediate ones. As a matter of conceptual fact, and also of historical, voluntarism shades into intellectualism. It is at this point that my reservations about the personalisation of the dispute start to take shape, for Duns Scotus, *Doctor Subtilis* to subsequent generations of scholastic writers, inhabits a rather shady part of the spectrum, a part in which the two categories apply to him in almost equal measure. Scotus is undoubtedly a voluntarist of sorts, but let us determine precisely what sort. I am sure that the usual modern account of his voluntarism fails to take due cognisance of some of his key pronouncements, and in consequence greatly underestimates the role he ascribes to intellect in the guidance of will.

This point derives particular significance from the fact that though Scotus is thought by some to be the leading exponent of voluntarist philosophy,[2] he is also thought to be a realist at least in respect of his teaching on universals. But how can he be a realist on that central topic given that voluntarism is so closely allied to nominalism? The first step to resolving this difficulty is to recognise slogans for what they are – alternatives to thought. Voluntarism, realism, and so on are very crude categories, each allowing room for systems of great variety and differing from each other in ways both gross and subtle. It is necessary to get inside Scotus's system, and to see in detail to what extent he deserves the title 'voluntarist' and to see indeed what the term means as applied to his ideas. Without some knowledge of the details we cannot properly understand his doctrine that will has primacy over intellect.

More immediately, discussion of whether it is will or intellect that has primacy presupposes that the two faculties are sufficiently distinct for either to have primacy over the other. Yet that presupposition is not free of difficulty. Two positions, one associated with Henry of Ghent (d. 1293), a master of theology at the University of Paris c. 1275–c. 1292, and the other associated with St Thomas Aquinas, have to be considered here, and the positions figure significantly in Scotus's philosophy since he constructs his own doctrine explicitly in opposition to those two others.[3]

Henry of Ghent is interpreted by Scotus as having identified will and intellect with each other and both with the soul. The pressure to make such an identification stems chiefly from the metaphysical intuition that mind has a special unity, one so great that it is impossible for any part of it to be really distinct from any other. If two parts were really distinct then it would be possible for one to exist without the other. But, to take just one example, it is absolutely impossible for there to be acts of will by a human agent where his intellect is not engaged; willing that does not involve at least the intellectual grasp of an end which is the object of the act of will, would be abstract will. And in reality there is no abstract will. Our acts of will are not willings without qualification, they are willings of some object grasped by intellect. Will is therefore in reality inseparable from intellect. What is the underlying metaphysical situation which explains this inseparability? Henry's reply is that though mind acts in different ways – it wills and it understands – it is a single principle of action, mind, which performs those distinct acts. According to this view, therefore, the fundamental metaphysical categories that should be deployed in discussions of mind are those of agent and act. We are dealing here with the oneness of the agent in relation to diverse acts, rather than the oneness of a substance which has a diversity of accidents.

It is true that Henry says that the powers of mind are really distinct from each other, but Scotus interprets him as using the term 'really' in a relative sense only. The theory that emerges is something subtle, but important for an understanding of Henry's philosophy of mind, and I should like to comment on it. Henry is saying that mind is related to acts of several distinct kinds. There are therefore a number of kinds of relation of which mind is an end point.[4] These relations are real. Or at any rate let us say that they have as much reality as Henry of Ghent ascribes to relations, as opposed to the things which form the termini of relations. Let us grant therefore that the relations in question, those between a mind and its diverse kinds of act, do have some sort of reality, even if it is a reality that is vicarious, in the sense that, in Henry's word, it is a reality 'contracted' from or drawn from the thing, the mind, to which the act is related as to its agent. Henry's claim that relations have a sort of reality is relevant to our purposes since it is his contention that the relations in which the acts of a mind stand to the mind are what powers of mind are. Intellect is thus a relation between a mind and its acts of understanding; will is a relation between a mind and its acts of willing; memory is a relation between a mind and its acts of remembering; imagination is a relation between a mind and its acts of imagining.

On this view it is no mistake to suppose that acts of willing and understanding are distinct from each other; neither is it a mistake to say that there are distinct powers of mind, so long as nothing more is meant than that mind performs distinct kinds of act and is therefore related to distinct kinds of act. The mistake which Henry of Ghent is concerned to expose is the mistake of referring these different sorts of act to different parts of mind, as if mind had a multiplicity of separable parts, when in reality it is an indivisible unity.

In contrast with Henry of Ghent's position is that of St Thomas Aquinas. As Scotus reads Aquinas the latter holds that intellect and will have a different kind of being from mind, for mind is the substance of which will and intellect are accidents. And will and intellect are also distinct from each other, being different accidents of mind.

It is plain that Scotus sees merit in each of these mutually opposed positions. For Henry of Ghent takes due notice of the fact that mind and its faculties form an unbreakable unity, and Aquinas is responsive to the fact that acts as different as willing and understanding must be referred to metaphysically distinct principles of action.

Scotus responds to the merit in each of these mutually incompatible positions by seeking a compromise between them. The compromise comes in the form of the deployment of his most distinctive concept, not one that he invented but one he made his own. It is that of the formal distinction, or more precisely the formal objective distinction (*distinctio formalis a parte rei*).[5] In order to be clear about Scotus's teaching on the relation between intellect and will, it is necessary to know how he deploys the distinction I have just mentioned. I shall therefore dwell on it for some moments.

Scotus deployed countless distinctions. Among them there is one, somewhat reflexive, between different sorts of distinction. Among the distinctions in common currency throughout the Middle Ages are the *distinctio realis* and the *distinctio logicalis*, the real distinction and the logical distinction. Two things are *really* distinct if the cessation of either does not imply the cessation of the other. On the other hand the distinction between the definitum and the definiens of a definition is merely *logical*. Thus something can be classified equally as a human being and as a rational animal, and the difference of classification is not based upon different features of the thing – the objective ground of its classification as a human being is really identical to the objective ground of its classification as a rational animal.

The question arises as to whether two things can be distinct in a more than merely logical way, yet without being really distinct. William Ockham, greatest of the medieval nominalists, answered in the negative, and attacked his fellow-Franciscan Scotus of the immediately preceding generation for giving an affirmative answer. The intermediate distinction Scotus deployed is the 'formal objective distinction'. He holds that in the human mind will and intellect are bound together in an absolutely unbreakable bond, absolute in the sense that not even God could annihilate one while preserving the other. In that sense they are not really distinct; that is, will and intellect are not distinct beings. Nevertheless they are not indistinguishable, for it is a matter of common experience that our will can say 'no' to whatever proposal intellect may commend to it. Yet if will and intellect are, in the sense just outlined, not really different, how are we to speak of the difference between them? Scotus calls them different 'formalities' of mind. A single reality can have several forms, say a tactile form and a visual form, simultaneously. The sheet of paper feels smooth to the touch, and it has a shiny white appearance. The smoothness, shininess, and whiteness are not distinct parts of the sheet of paper, but different forms that the one reality, the sheet, takes. In this context Scotus speaks not of forms but of formalities. His doctrine is that the single reality, mind, has simultaneously several distinct formalities, a will and an intellect, a memory and an imagination. Mind is the active principle in us. Some of its acts take the form of willing, and some of understanding, some of its acts take the form of remembering and some of imagining. And the act takes the form it does because the agent, mind, takes the form of a willer, or an understander, and so on. What Scotus refuses to lose sight of is the fact that it is one and the same identical mind that takes these various forms. Its oneness is not in the least compromised by the fact that mind takes these various forms.

In making sense of the formal distinction we should hold on to the context of its formulation. It is not a distinction plucked randomly out of the air, but is instead forced upon Scotus by the need to find a compromise position between the unacceptable and mutually incompatible positions of Henry of Ghent and St Thomas Aquinas. Since the distinction between will and intellect is formal, yet grounded in reality, Scotus can maintain both that mind is one and that the very different sorts of act, of will on the one hand and intellect on the other, must be referred to different principles of action.

One further distinction must here be made, that between two sorts of will.[6] We need to be clear about these two sorts, for when Scotus ascribes primacy to will over intellect, it is just one of these sorts of will that is at issue.

There are certain imperatives with which we seem by our very nature to be confronted. Most fundamentally the organism demands its continued existence. We can of course decide to reject the demand, but if we do then we do not silence that natural voice within us; instead we overrule it. The organism wills one thing, and we will to the contrary, and on such an occasion the organism might lose. But there are many other things also that we will by our nature; nourishment, warmth, sleep, and so on. All these things contribute to our perfection, the perfection of the natural organism. I am speaking here of its flourishing or well-functioning. The principle in us by virtue of which we have a natural tendency or bias or inclination to our perfection is in a sense a principle of passivity. For when, if ever, we give nature its head and follow through such tendencies we are living according to nature and nature's laws; we are responding passively to nature as it is articulated in us.

But there is within us another principle, this time an active one, which is also termed 'will'. This latter principle is exercised when we do not passively sit back and let nature take its course, but instead we interfere, as we almost always do, with the orderly working out of nature. We stand against nature and either will contrarily to it, or we will consistently with it but not in virtue of being compelled by nature. That there is such a principle in us is evidenced by the fact that a person can overcome his natural fear of death, and will his death. The fear remains, that voice of nature within us, willing the organism to do whatever is necessary to ensure its survival. And yet we can take a stand against our nature by saying 'no' to its demand. The will by which we reject life and instead go voluntarily towards death, is clearly a different principle of action within us from the natural principle by which we will to live. If the latter sort of will should be called 'natural will', what should the former sort be called? Scotus says that it is a 'free will'.

There are two reasons, one negative, the other positive, for calling it free. The first is plain, namely, that it is *free from nature* in this sense at least, that it is not determined to act by any act of nature. To say that an act of will is determined by natural law would be to say precisely that the act is unfree. This is in an obvious sense a negative characterisation of will.

We should not be taken in by the term 'negative'. Negative freedom, though negative, is an awesome thing. Let us pause to gain a sense of this. Contrast on the one hand the whole system of nature in its infinite power, with on the other hand us human beings, finite, all too finite, almost nothing at all in the presence of the overwhelming power of nature. Yet 'overwhelming' is not quite the right word here, and it is important to see why. The natural world does not determine me to lift this pencil. Left to the devices of nature neither this pencil nor my hand would rise. But they are not left to the devices of nature. They are left to my devices, and I will to lift the pencil. It is as if whenever I exert my will I take on the whole system of nature and win. If indeed nature is infinite in its power, then my ability to stay at a distance from nature, so that there is a kind of space between myself and it, and act in a way that is not determined by it – this implies that my own will also is, in a certain sense, infinite in its power. Far from being overwhelmed by nature I am so powerful as to be able to use nature to secure ends which it has not determined for me. It is with this power in mind that I speak of the awesomeness of the power of the human will.

That however, as just stated, is to characterise free will negatively; we are saying what it is free from. But Scotus is equally interested in the positive characterisation of such a will; and in developing the positive side he employs a distinction between rational and irrational powers.[7] He takes the distinction from Aristotle,[8] but what he makes of it is more than, and perhaps entirely other than, anything intended by Aristotle. In Scotus's hands the distinction becomes that between a power which can produce opposite effects, this being a rational power, and that which can produce only one effect, this being irrational. For example, our free will is rational since in one and the same circumstance we can will to walk and equally will to run; we can will to speak and equally will to be silent. A fire, on the other hand, is not a rational power, since it heats the object that is adjacent to it, and it can do nothing about that. That is its nature, and it is constrained entirely by nature's laws.

The formulation of this distinction needs to be tightened up, as Scotus was well aware. To say that a free will, a rational power, can produce opposite effects is not to imply that it can produce them simultaneously. Such an act would be impossible. It is to say instead that at the moment it produces one effect, it could equally, and in the very same circumstance, have produced another effect instead.

But this concept of a free will is not plain sailing. How should we deal with the argument that if a free will is equally able, from within its own resources, to produce opposite effects, then which of the opposites it produces is not explained simply in terms of the power of the will; the fact that that particular effect rather than any other was produced must therefore be explained by reference to some further power, for example, desire. And if it must be explained in some such way then the free will is, after all, not equally able to produce each of the opposite effects. Indeed by itself it apparently cannot produce either of them.

The reply to this criticism of the claim that a free will *qua* rational power can produce opposite effects is that the criticism is based upon a misunderstanding of the nature of free will. What makes it free is precisely that without any further determination, and in particular without input from any further psychological power, will is able to determine, from within its own resources, which of the various possible effects equally within its power it should will into actuality.

I shall now change the direction of my attack on the distinction between rational and irrational powers, and shall consider the claim that the distinction can be reduced to an absurdity. Scotus holds that a rational power can produce opposite effects, and instances will; and on the other hand an irrational power can produce only one effect. An attack could be mounted against this account on the grounds that there are many things that we do not think of as rational or as free which can nevertheless produce opposite effects, and those things therefore must after all be free. Consider the sun as an example of an irrational power, a power which is in no sense free. Yet as regards its effects on our corner of the universe, it blackens and it bleaches, it promotes life and it also kills. In other words the sun produces opposite effects, and therefore counts as a rational power, and therefore is free. Yet it manifestly is not free. What, then, has gone wrong with the account?

The answer is that the sun can indeed produce opposite effects, but those effects are not equally open to it. In precisely those circumstances in which it blackens a given object it could not bleach it. In precisely those circumstances in which it fosters life in a given object it could not kill it. When Scotus speaks about a power being rational in the sense that it can produce opposite effects, he means that in the identical circumstance in which it produces one of those opposite effects it could equally produce the other.

In order to provide further clarification of the crucial distinction between rational and irrational powers I should like to follow through one further possible line of attack on it. If will is truly free then it must, as we have seen, be able to will opposites. Will can certainly will good *qua* good, and hence it should be able to will the opposite to that, namely, evil *qua* evil. But surely it cannot do that. Surely whenever a person wills evil it is for the sake of a greater good, or it is evil perceived by the agent as good. Hence will is determined to will what it perceives to be good, say, happiness. In that case it is determined to a single effect, and in that case it is not free.

Scotus's reply to this difficulty is to concede the premises but to resist the conclusion that will is determined to a single effect and therefore is not free. His reply is that faced with a good, say happiness, will can will it, or nill it, or simply refuse to choose. It is true that it cannot respond by willing misery, an evil, for its own sake. But it still has an alternative available to it, that of doing nothing. Since will, faced with the possibility of happiness, can refrain from willing happiness, it is not determined to a single effect. Hence the argument under consideration does not prove that will is not free.[9]

But if our will is free, what role remains for our intellect in determining which acts we shall perform? Can intellect play any role without encroaching on our freedom? And if it cannot, then is our freedom not bought at the cost of a profound irrationality at the heart of all our acts? These are the questions I shall address in the next lecture, when I investigate the doctrine of the primacy of the will.

NOTES

1. In this chapter and the next I make use of the invaluable selection of Scotus's writings: *Duns Scotus on the Will and Morality*, Selected and translated with an Introduction by Allan B. Wolter, O.F.M. For an extended discussion of the topic of this chapter see B. M. Bonansea, 'Duns Scotus's voluntarism' in J. K. Ryan and B. M. Bonansea (eds), *John Duns Scotus 1265–1965*. That paper is reprinted as chapter two of B. M. Bonansea O.F.M., *Man and his Approach to God in John Duns Scotus*.

2. Another contender for this title is Immanuel Kant. For his contribution to the debate see especially *Critique of Practical Reason*, Pt. 1, Bk. 2, Ch. 3, Sect. 3, and L. W. Beck, *A Commentary on Kant's Critique of Practical Reason*, London 1960, pp. 249–50.

3. A key text is *Opus Oxoniense* II, d. 16, quaestio unica; in Scotus, *Opera Omnia*, ed. Wadding, vol. XIII, pp. 23a–59b. Scotus there discusses a number of opposed positions including those of Henry of Ghent and Aquinas. Scotus represents Aquinas's position thus: 'Intellectus et voluntas sunt duae potentiae realiter distinctae inter se, et ab essentia animae (de memoria modo non loquor); passiones enim animae sunt illae duae potentiae et proprietates, et accidentia fluentia ab ipsa; accidens autem realiter differt a substantia', *ibid.*, p. 24a–b (See Aquinas, *Summa Theologiae* Pt. 1, q. 77: De his quae pertinent ad potentias animae in generali). Scotus represents Henry's position thus: 'Alii dicunt quod potentiae animae sunt idem essentiae animae, distinctae tamen inter se realitate relativa, ita quod potentia animae non dicit nisi esse cum respectu coassumpto ... quod anima secundum se comparatur ad diversos actus, sunt in anima diversi respectus qui dicuntur diversae potentiae, et per huiusmodi diversos respectus determinatur ad diversos actus', *ibid.*, pp. 35b–36a.

4. For Henry of Ghent on relations, see Mark G. Henninger, S.J., *Relations: Medieval Theories 1250–1325*, pp. 40–58.

5. Scotus's position is stated unambiguously: 'Sic ergo possumus accipere de intellectu et voluntate, quae non sunt partes essentiales animae, sed sunt unitive contenta in anima quasi passiones eius, propter quas anima est operativa, non quod sint essentia eius formaliter, sed sunt formaliter distinctae, idem tamen identice et unitive ut in *Primo Libro* probatum est de attributis divinis', *Opera Omnia,* ed. Wadding, vol. XIII, pp. 43b–44a.

6. Wolter, *Duns Scotus on the Will and Morality*, pp. 180–3.

7. For Scotus on rational and irrational powers see Wolter, *Duns Scotus on the Will and Morality*, pp. 144–73. Wolter's text is a revised version of Scotus, *Opera Omnia*, ed. Wadding, vol. VII, pp. 606–17.

8. Aristotle, *Metaphysics* IX, 1046 b 1–4: 'It is clear that some potencies will be nonrational but others will be with reason. Hence all the arts or productive sciences are potencies.'

9. See Wolter, *op. cit.*, pp. 144–5, 192–5, esp. pp. 194–5: 'Hence, when [will] is shown happiness, it can refrain from acting at all. In regard to any object, then, will is able not to will it or nill it, and can suspend itself from eliciting any act in particular with regard to this or that. And this is something anyone can experience in himself when someone proffers some good. Even if it is presented as something to be considered and willed, one can turn away from it and not elicit any act in its regard.'

Lecture 3

The primacy of the will

THE UNREMITTING emphasis, in the writings of Duns Scotus, on the concept of will is part of the reason why he has come to be regarded as an extreme voluntarist. Another concept which plays a pivotal role within his system is that of love. Its centrality tends, if anything, to reinforce the perception of him as an extreme voluntarist, for he locates love in the will. Love, in short, is seen as an act of will, a point which at first blush may sound strange, though not so strange when seen within the context of the teaching that we are commanded to love God, and that we would not be commanded to do what we cannot will to do. Therefore we can will to love God, and therefore a voluntarist theologian may be expected to emphasise the role of love in the religious consciousness. And that is precisely what Scotus does.

In this lecture I shall seek to argue that Scotus's reputation as an extreme voluntarist is unwarranted. It has certainly been held by some that Scotus assigns a very much smaller role than does Thomas Aquinas to intellect in the direction of will, but, as I shall argue, Scotus in fact assigns a major and crucially important role to intellect as director of will. He does indeed insist on the freedom of will, but nevertheless sees will as always, or almost always, acting as intellect directs. And this is not an extreme form of voluntarism. It is hardly voluntarism at all. I shall explore here Scotus's teachings on will and shall attend to relevant aspects of his teachings on intellect, the power with which will is routinely contrasted. I hope that in the light of the discussion on these two powers we shall be better able to identify Duns Scotus's stance regarding the doctrine of the primacy of will.

In the first lecture I emphasised the fact that Scotus was a Franciscan friar. There is a popular image of Franciscans derived largely, I think, from the familiar stories of St Francis preaching to the birds and animals of the forest. He is seen as a person in a close bond, a bond of love, with all nature. This image of St Francis is, as no doubt it should be, in close accord with the main thrust of what is thought of as characteristically Franciscan theology. Among the guiding principles of that theology are the doctrines that God's relation to Himself is a relation of love, that the second and third persons of the Trinity were produced through the inner dynamic of that divine love, and that the world was created, and is maintained, by God in an act of love. From all of which it follows that in so far as the emotional form of our stance in relation to the created order is one of love, our lives are an *imitatio Dei*, that imitation of the divine that was commended by all medieval theologians as the highest form of existence available to us creatures by nature. St Francis was thought by many to have been special in the fulness of his embodiment of that ideal.

The theological ideas I have just formulated are presented in detail by Richard Scot in his *De Trinitate*, written while living in the Abbey of St Victor in Paris during the latter part of the twelfth century, and they were absorbed into the Franciscan system of thought almost at the start. It is easy to see why those ideas might be peculiarly congenial to St Francis himself, for whom love was at the centre of the universe. And those same ideas must have formed a dominant part of the educational ethos of Duns Scotus's childhood. Scotus, as we have seen, emphasises the closeness of the relation between love and the will, arguing that will is the power within which love is located. I shall shortly consider the meaning of this doctrine, but it may here be noted that in view of Scotus's emphasis upon God as the God of love, and in view also of his doctrine that will is the place of love, it is to be expected that his theological enquiries will focus upon God's will rather than upon His intellect.

Scotus's teachings on the will of God, and particularly on the infinitude of His will, have important implications for the whole enterprise of natural theology. Perhaps I should feel more guilty than I do, lecturing under the aegis of Lord Gifford, in arguing that if we place sufficient emphasis upon the concept of God's infinite will we may have to conclude that it is impossible for natural theology ever to succeed in proving anything whatever about God. It is my own view, and not stated merely out of respect for Lord Gifford, that it is much too early to think about abandoning the discipline of natural theology, but the particular problem associated with the concept of God's infinite will should here be stated in view of the fact that the problem is thoroughly Scotist.

At the heart of natural theology is the idea that a suitably angled investigation of the natural order can lead to the conclusion that God exists, and can lead also to insights into His nature. As regards one large aspect of this theological programme, let us suppose that the relation of God to the created world is somewhat like the relation of a human artificer to an artefact that he has made. It is not in doubt that we can learn about a human artificer by a consideration of his artefacts. Examination of a violin and of a statue yields knowledge of the aesthetic values and the manipulative skills of the violin maker and the sculptor. We might even think that we can learn a great deal about the artificer by considering what he has made.

If the relation between God and the world is somewhat like that between the artificer and his artefacts, why not say that we can learn something about God the Creator by a consideration of the created order? Perhaps we could say that, but it is difficult to do so if God has an infinite will. Let us grant that God created our world by an act of will. We must bear in mind Scotus's doctrine that a free will is able to produce opposite effects. That is, in the very circumstances in which it produces the effect that it does produce it could equally produce an opposite effect instead. This is true even of a finite will. If God's will is infinite then whatever world he creates he must have been able to create an infinitely different world, and he might in fact have created an infinite number of such worlds no less different from each other than any one of them is from ours, worlds utterly inaccessible to the human intellect. I do not find this idea bizarre. What limit, after all, can I suppose God's will to have once I suppose Him able to create our world?

The crucial logical point for our purposes is that God might have created another world with features unimaginably different from the features that our world displays through which we seek to understand the divine nature. This has to be granted once we take seriously the concept of the infinitude of the divine will. But the implication is that what we can learn about God by investigation of our world is vanishingly little compared with what there is to learn about Him. And it is irrelevant whether God has in fact created other worlds. The point that matters is that the possibility of His having created others cannot be ruled out if we say that He has an infinite will. The conclusion is not that we can learn nothing at all about God by investigation of the natural order. No doubt we can learn more than nothing, but not by much.

What has just been said about the perceptual universe can equally be said about what is sometimes termed the moral universe. Since God's will is infinite we cannot rule out the possibility that in some other world He has revealed a set of commandments different from, and indeed incompatible with, the set of commandments revealed to Moses at Sinai. What then can we learn about God by investigation of the Decalogue?

I believe that Scotus saw as well as anyone ever could the extent to which the infinity of the divine will is an obstacle to our learning about God by an examination of the created order. We subsequently find the same emphasis on the divine will in the writings of his great Franciscan successor, William Ockham. And the idea that God is, in the sense just outlined, concealed from us behind His infinite will, may well have been a contributory factor to vital developments in the fifteenth and sixteenth centuries, in particular the encroachment of humanism. The path to characteristic humanist endeavours is easily described. If we can read off so little about God by a consideration of the natural order, what is left to us as a source of knowledge about Him? The answer is: the Bible and its authoritative interpreters. But in that case it is necessary to have a critical edition of the Bible, both the Hebrew Bible and the Greek New Testament. The serious deficiencies of the Vulgate were more and more exposed to the light of linguistic scholarship, and those deficiencies were a major spur to the studies of the classical languages, Hebrew and Greek, no less than Latin, studies which were so central to the programme of the humanists.

I am not setting at Scotus's door the responsibility for these great changes as Europe moved into the age of Renaissance humanism and the Protestant Reformation. But I have no doubt that he was a major contributor to the developments that took place in that direction. Of course, once a writer's ideas are in the public domain they are available to be appropriated by all sorts of people with all sorts of perspectives and motivations. As a result, those ideas can work themselves out in history and emerge in forms which would appal their progenitors. Scotus may indeed, as has been argued persuasively, have had a significant influence on Calvin,[1] but we should not conclude that Scotus was any kind of pre-Calvin Calvinist.

The doctrine that God has an infinite will gives rise to a question concerning constraints on our ability to learn of our obligations. It may be argued that, as implied earlier, if God has an infinite will then he could reveal to us any one of an infinite number of sets of commandments, even a set incompatible with the Decalogue, and consequently the only way we could learn how we ought to live is by consideration of the revealed law. The doctrine that we cannot by the exercise of our unaided reason work out how we ought to live is commonly ascribed to Scotus. But in fact that doctrine was never taught by Scotus himself, who on the contrary speaks at length about the rational basis of the Decalogue.

It is appropriate to present here a sample of the evidence regarding Scotus's view on the rationality of morality. There are many suitable passages. The one selected has been chosen because of its ready accessiblity.[2]

Scotus asks whether all the precepts of the Decalogue belong to the Law of Nature, and begins his reply by offering reasons for saying 'no'. The first reason is this: Precepts of the Law of Nature, whether practical principles known from their terms to be true or whether deduced from those principles, are necessarily true. Not even God can grant us dispensation from such precepts because God cannot make false what is necessarily true. Yet God granted dispensation from the prohibitions on killing and theft. Therefore those commandments do not belong to the Law of Nature. The second reason is this: Paul the Apostle declares: 'I did not know sin except through the Law. For I would not have known [the sinfulness of] covetousness if the Law had not said: "Thou shalt not covet".' But if something is known to be required or prohibited by the Law of Nature, it can be known even if not written. Hence 'Thou shalt not covet' does not belong to the Law of Nature. But if the precepts of the Decalogue do not belong to the Law of Nature then their bindingness can only be due to the fact that they are commanded by God, from which it follows that the value of a life lived in accordance with the Decalogue is an object of divine will. The value is held in existence by an act of divine will. Hence in order to know how we ought to live we must determine God's will by a study of Scripture.

This is however not Scotus's view of the relation between the Decalogue and the Law of Nature. His starting point is that there are two ways in which precepts can belong to the Law of Nature. One of them is as set out earlier, that is, they belong either as first practical principles known from their terms or as conclusions following necessarily from such principles. Precepts of either kind are said to belong in the strictest sense (*strictissime*) to the Law of Nature. Being necessary truths, God cannot grant us dispensation from them. The commandments from the fourth ('Honour your father and your mother') to the tenth do not belong to the Law in the strictest sense, for disobedience of them is compatible with the agent's attainment of the ultimate end, beatitude.

On the other hand the first two commandments on the first table of the Law, 'You shall have no gods other than me' and 'You shall not take the name of your God in vain', are otherwise placed in relation to God's will. Scotus declares: 'They belong to the Law of Nature, taking "Law of Nature" strictly . . . And in consequence God could not give dispensation from them in such a way that a person would be able to do the opposite to one or the other prohibition.' Scotus expresses doubt about the third commandment: 'Remember the Sabbath day to keep it holy.' On one interpretation, though not on another, it does perhaps belong to the Law of Nature in the strict sense of the phrase. But in any case Scotus is unequivocal about the first two commandments of the Decalogue – their existence is not a product of the divine will. God is infinitely lovable, and it is this fact about Him and not the fact of our having been commanded that is the ground of our obligation to love Him. Our loving Him has therefore a value antecedent to an act of the divine will, and the value is therefore neither brought into existence nor sustained in existence by an act of that same will. Put negatively, God cannot, absolutely cannot, command us to hate Him. Scotus interprets the first two commandments as following necessarily from the requirement that we love God.

Scotus does however note a second way in which things can belong to the Law of Nature, namely by being very much consonant (*multum consona*) with it, even though they do not follow necessarily from first practical principles which are known from their terms and which are known necessarily by every intellect. Scotus comments: 'In respect of this second way, it is certain that all the commandments of the second table also belong to the Law of Nature, since their rightness is very consonant indeed (*valde consonat*) with those necessarily known first practical principles.' It is because the commandments of the second table do not belong in the strict sense to the Law of Nature that God can grant a dispensation from them.

As regards the argument that the commandments of the Decalogue cannot belong to the Law of Nature since Paul the Apostle affirmed that it was only when he learned the law prohibiting covetousness that he learned of the sinfulness of covetousness, Scotus's reply is as follows: 'Even if it were possible to conclude that some act of covetousness were against the Law of Nature, nevertheless the fact that covetousness is against the Law of Nature was not known to corrupt men, and hence it was necessary to explain, whether by means of the law that was handed down or by other means, that acts of covetousness are prohibited by commandments of the second table. And it has been conceded that as regards such commandments, they are not known in themselves.'

I conclude that Scotus believes that we can after all by the exercise of our reason, and without relying solely on religious authoritative texts, learn something about how we ought to live. To this extent he teaches that there is a rational basis to morality, and to this extent the attribution of moral irrationalism to him is false.

Nevertheless we must acknowledge that the commandments on the second table, though 'very consonant' with the Law of Nature, do not follow necessarily from it. God could therefore have promulgated different commandments from the ones He did promulgate for us, and perhaps has in fact promulgated different Decalogues, even for beings like us, in other worlds – though these other Decalogues could not contain the negations of the first two commandments. I say that Scotus recognised this as a possibility, even though he also thought that God would not, though He could, promulgate commandments which were not consonant with the nature of those who were to live by them. The underlying metaphysical point remains, that God, being infinitely free, could produce an infinite variety of codes of conduct, and even if we know to whom a given code is directed we are unable to deduce what it will contain, beyond the fact that it cannot contain either the commandment that God not be loved or any necessary implicate of that commandment. In this respect we are as little able to learn about God by a consideration of the moral universe as we are by a consideration of the perceptual.

I shall now focus more precisely on the issue of Scotus's voluntarism, and shall begin by deploying the formal objective distinction (*distinctio formalis a parte rei*). In Lecture Two we observed Scotus arguing that it is precisely that distinction that has to be made between intellect and will, for though the two mental powers are not different realities in the one mind, the distinction that we draw between them is grounded in reality – to use Scotus's technical term, they are different *formalities*. That is, mind can take different forms, one in so far as it is a willer, and another in so far as it is an understander. Since the two powers are formally, and not merely logically, distinct they are sufficiently different for it to be appropriate to ask which of them has primacy. As a first

41

step towards answering this question let us consider two positions at opposite ends of a spectrum. One is extreme intellectualism and the other extreme voluntarism.

The intellectualist position first. According to it will by itself is blind, and requires a judgment of intellect if an act of will is to occur. Thus intellect presents will with an object, a plan of action, and will wills that plan into reality. A corollary of the doctrine that will is blind is that it can do nothing by itself, and requires direction from intellect if it is to act. We are not to think here of a blind act of will as an act which is somehow performed though not directed to any particular goal. The intellectualist would say that on the contrary a will that wills blindly is a will that wills nothing. To will nothing is not to will at all. Hence blind willing is not one form of willing among others; it is instead not any form of willing.

But the fact, if it be one, that will can do nothing by itself, does not imply that will plays no role in action. We can still say that the cause of an act, the reason why we go in one direction rather than in another, and why we go anywhere rather than nowhere, is that will has been directed by intellect. It is possible to construct a concept of freedom which is compatible with this version of events. Thus to say that an act is freely performed is to say that a will wills it under the direction of intellect. The will itself is free, and the cause of the freely willed act is the intellect's directive.

It is not entirely fanciful to suppose that some philosophers have held this position. St Thomas Aquinas speaks in terms very similar to the ones I have just employed. For example, he tells us that so far as what is at issue is the subject of freedom, that is, what has freedom as an attribute, the root of freedom is will, but so far as what is at issue is the cause of freedom, then the root of freedom is reason.[3] On Scotus's interpretation of this position, it is saying that the free activity of will is fully accounted for by events on the side of intellect, and in Scotus's view this cannot be correct; it involves a misappropriation of the term 'freedom'.

In effect what is being called 'freedom' is determinism under another name. It is determinism by intellect. But intellectual determinism is not the less determinism for being of the intellectual variety. In brief, how can will be free if it is bound to do whatever it is told to by intellect? It is not even vicariously free, owing such freedom as it has to being under the direction of a free faculty, for no-one supposes the faculty of intellect itself to be free. If freedom is to be located anywhere it must be in will and not in intellect. I am not saying that Aquinas is committed to the version of intellectualism just outlined, though there is no doubt that he leaves himself open to being understood in the way Scotus understands him. And according to that understanding of the matter one might almost speak of the will as totally appropriated by intellect. Will has been fully intellectualised, left with nothing to do beyond what it is told.

However, if the doctrine at the intellectualist extremity of the spectrum is unacceptable, then the doctrine at the opposite, the voluntarist, extremity seems no less so. For extreme voluntarism declares that will acts freely to the extent that it is not responding to the deliverances of reason. This position is no more acceptable than its extreme opposite, for it is contrary to experience. We observe as a matter of course that people do act in ways sanctioned by reason, at any rate sanctioned by their reason, and their acting in a rational way is not reckoned as evidence of unfreedom. In particular it is not regarded as evidence of intellectual determinism.

Clearly what is required is a position between the two extremes, and Scotus is the very voice of moderation on this matter. His commitment to a compromise position is already implicit in his metaphysical doctrine of the formal distinction between will and intellect, according to which the two faculties are not distinct realities in the mind but on the contrary have an irrefragable unity of being. In that sense, will and intellect are the same reality, for it is one and the same mind that wills and understands. Since not even God can separate the two powers in reality, Scotus leaves himself no logical room to argue that will can act as if intellect does not exist.

Closely related to this doctrine is the dictum that nothing is willed that is not previously known – *Nihil volitum quin praecognitum*. We cannot will without willing something. There is thus in the mind of the willer a concept of what is willed, a plan of action, something formed by an act of intellect, that is to be put into effect by means of an act of will. Scotus is explicit on the closeness of willing and understanding. Speaking about the necessary relation between the two, he writes: 'On account of that necessary relation an act of will cannot be caused by the faculty of will unless an act of understanding has already been caused by the intellect.'[4]

That an act of will cannot occur without a prior exercise of intellect, and cannot occur without due account being taken by will of the content of the intellectual act, does not however imply that the act of will is fully determined by that prior intellectual act. There are degrees of influence that fall short of full determination, and it is such a limited influence that is at issue in this context. Scotus's phrase is *pondus et inclinatio*.[5] The deliverances of intellect carry weight with will and incline it; but not more than that. No such deliverance can carry so much weight that will finds it irresistible. When the weight is irresistible will is simply not engaged at all, because for will to be engaged is for it to act as will, and an act of will is a free act. In this context to speak of will as free is to say that it has the power to produce opposite effects. Thus whatever it does now it could in these very same circumstances have done otherwise.

Scotus does not baulk at the idea of will being coerced, relatively speaking, as happens when right reason informs a person that if he does not perform an act of a kind that he would not otherwise be inclined to perform there might be a much worse outcome than if he does perform the act. So he performs it, an act which is in a relative sense forced, and he performs it, as Scotus puts it, *secundum rectam rationem* – in accordance with right reason. But in this case will is free. The agent could, in those very circumstances, have acted otherwise. But being a reasonable person, he went in the direction dictated by right reason.

I am not concerned here to argue for the claim that we do have the power to produce opposite effects. I merely say that if we do not then, at least on Scotus's view of the matter, we are not free agents. In particular an extreme intellectualist account of will, according to which acts of will are fully determined by the deliverances of intellect, would not be, on Scotus's reckoning, an account of *free* will at all. Consequently, if we have a free will we must be able to stand sufficiently far back from any directive of our intellect to be able to reject it. Even if we do not reject it, and would be judged crazy if we did, the possibility of rejecting it remains open to us, right up to the moment we act. And even when performing the act thus sanctioned by intellect the possibility of curtailing the act, however crazy it would be to do so, remains open to us. That a particular possibility in our power is a crazy one for us to actualise, is no doubt going to be our reason or part of our reason for not actualising it. But that is not to say that we *cannot* actualise it; it is simply our reason why we *will* not. That is what it is for intellect to have *pondus et inclinatio*, to carry weight and to dispose, in its relation to will. As just noted, to say it is impossible for us to reject the judgment of intellect is to deny our freedom.

We might however wonder whether the judgment of intellect really can carry weight with will if will does not itself include an intellectual component. For surely weighing up the judgment of intellect is itself an intellectual act, and hence if will can perform such an act is it not itself an intellectual power? And here we cannot ignore Scotus's teaching that will and intellect are the same reality, both being identical with mind. But if will and intellect are one then has will not thereby been intellectualised? And in that case since intellect is not free neither is will, for on this hypothesis there is nothing more to will than intellect. That is, to attribute properties of intellect to will is to imply intellectual determinism.

On the other hand, if will does not have an intellectual component then why should judgments of intellect make any difference to it? And if they make no difference then surely our freely willed acts would be random. But, as noted earlier, experience teaches us that our acts, especially those we regard as free, do not appear to be random. And in all his philosophising Scotus never loses sight of the deliverances of experience.

These are difficult questions, and ones I think that Scotus has in view when he applies his concept of the formal objective distinction to his account of the relation between will and intellect. The two powers are not in all respects identical – they are after all two powers, not one, each power having the metaphysical status of a formality of mind. And this distinction between them is sufficient to allow will freedom of manoeuvre in its dealings with intellect and with all other powers of mind.

The human mind has distinct forms, of a willer, a thinker, a recollecter, an imaginer, somewhat as we might say that a single literary work has the form of a historical novel, a love story, a political tract, and a social satire. There is nothing odd in the idea that a single work could be all these things at once, that is, that it could simultaneously have all these *forms*, and I think it is helpful to use this kind of literary model to make sense of Scotus's idea that mind has a number of different forms or 'formalities'. This might be understood in a purely functional way. That is, it could be taken to mean no more than that mind is able to perform acts of various kinds, such as thinking and willing. But it is plain that Scotus means something metaphysical, and not merely functional, by his talk about formalities. It is because mind has certain forms – this being a metaphysical fact about it – that it is able to perform acts of these various sorts. Its having these forms is not simply its being

45

able to perform the acts. The various forms that mind has, its powers of will and intellect, that make the different sorts of act possible, are its 'formalities'.

William Ockham, the greatest Franciscan thinker of the generation following Scotus, rejected Scotus's concept of formalities, removing them with the aid of his Razor, which is a methodological principle rather than, as it is normally represented, a metaphysical one. Ockham saw neither need for formalities, nor in the last analysis any sense in them. It is easy to see how the argument between the two philosophers is bound to go. Ockham declares that mind is able to will and to understand, and that its being able to do these things is all that is meant by the powers of mind. If it is suggested that there is some feature that mind must have in virtue of which it is able to perform these different sorts of act, Ockham will want to know why we need to take this extra step. What are these features? We do not, after all, experience them in any shape or form. What we are aware of, all that we are aware of that is relevant in this context, is that we do in fact perform acts of will and of understanding.

Scotus's reply to this position must be that nothing can function as it does without its having certain features that permit it to function in that way. It may be obvious what the features are in virtue of which it can perform its characteristic acts, it may not be, but whether or not we know what the features are is irrelevant to the fact that the thing must have them. This is as true of human minds as it is of human bodies and of all other sorts of bodies. The human mind is able to will and to understand. It must be in virtue of features of mind that it is able to perform acts of these two varieties. The relevant features, which we call the powers of will and intellect, have the metaphysical status of 'formalities'. This is the term Scotus uses to signify whatever it is that something has in virtue of which it is able to perform its characteristic acts. We do not need to have experienced a formality to know that it exists.

These metaphysical facts about will and intellect enable Scotus to conclude that the real identity of the two powers in the one human mind prevents our free acts from being random, and the formal distinctness of the powers ensures that our free acts are not wholly determined by intellect. Will determines itself, though always in the light of a judgment of intellect.

To adapt a common phrase: 'Intellect proposes but will disposes'. The last word lies with will, and will is no slave of intellect, even though it is sometimes driven very hard by it. That a directive of intellect can never simply be ignored is acknowledged by Scotus when he writes: 'It is difficult for will not to be inclined towards the final judgment of practical reason, but it is not impossible.'[6] This is voluntarism only in so far as it acknowledges that will is a self-determining power, but anyone who believes in a free will is, in that sense and to that extent, a voluntarist. But this minimal kind of voluntarism falls very far short of the kind that has been attributed to Scotus, according to which will is free to will in total disregard of intellect. This is not just a matter of will being able to override or overrule intellect, but of simply ignoring it. Scotus did not believe this possible. In so far as this extreme voluntarism is taught in the name of Scotus, and is part of Scotism, Scotus is no Scotist.

In the previous lecture I spoke about voluntarism and intellectualism on the one hand and nominalism and realism on the other. Voluntarism and intellectualism are doctrines within the philosophy of mind, and concern especially the question of which of the mental faculties has primacy. Nominalism and intellectualism are metaphysical doctrines concerning the mode of existence of given objects. We observed that voluntarists tend towards nominalism, and intellectualists towards realism. A question was then posed as to how Scotus could be a voluntarist and a realist at the same time. Having posed it I warned against using slogans as an alternative to thought. The technical terms deployed in this area had to be investigated. We have, since then, investigated, and are now half way to an answer to the question of how Scotus can be both a voluntarist and a realist. What we have unearthed is the fact that his voluntarism is minimal; it could indeed be described as the maximal sort of intellectualism compatible with the doctrine of free will. I hope to argue elsewhere that Scotus's realism is as minimal as his voluntarism.

We should not lose sight of the fact that realism and nominalism are doctrines on a spectrum, as also are the doctrines of intellectualism and voluntarism. I believe that Scotus performs the wonderfully skilful feat of standing in dynamic equilibrium right on the centre point of each spectrum. Indeed I have now produced arguments for concluding, at least tentatively, that these two spectra are so closely related that it would be difficult logically speaking to be at the centre of one without being at the centre of the other.

Yet if Scotus is a centrist, how can he ascribe primacy to will over intellect? Should he not give them equal weight? The answer is 'no'.

Part of the reason for this answer lies outside philosophy, and inside the kind of theology we associate especially with Franciscans. Typically, Franciscans subscribe to the doctrine of the primacy of love. Love is superior to knowledge and, especially, love of God is superior to knowledge of Him. If *per impossibile* we could love God without knowing Him and know God without loving Him, it would be better to love God than to know Him. This has immediate implications for the primacy of will, since love is located in will and not in intellect. If the highest act of which we are capable is an act of will then will has primacy over intellect.

Some might baulk at the idea that love is located in will, for if the doctrine has any meaning at all it must be that we exercise a measure of voluntary control over our acts of love. Yet it is not difficult to defend the claim. Love is necessarily directed to an object. Remove the object and the act ceases. If therefore we judge that our love for a given object is illicit, that the object is in some way unfitted for an emotional stance of that form, then the love can be removed by the act, which is subject to our will, of averting our gaze from the object. If on the contrary we judge that an object is worthy of our love, then the love can be induced or intensified by the act, which is subject to our will, of focusing our attention upon the object. In the first case as a result of an act of will we ceased to love, and in the second case as a result of such an act we came to love. On this basis there seems adequate grounds for speaking of love as subject to voluntary control, or, to use another idiom, to speak of will as the place of love.

Yet this premiss may not be sufficient to bear the weight of the conclusion that will, rather than intellect, has primacy among the powers of mind. Let us return to the principle: *Nihil volitum quin praecognitum*, and consider it in light of the argument that it is intellect that causes acts of will and not will that causes acts of intellect. The cause has primacy in relation to the effect, and therefore intellect, and not will, has primacy in the human mind. We must accept, in line with Scotus's teaching, that intellectual acts cause acts of will in the sense that nothing can be willed without the intellect having first conceived the plan that is then willed. And it surely follows that intellect does after all have primacy. Nevertheless, before accepting this conclusion it is necessary to ask whether it is possible for will to cause acts of intellect.

In his approach to this question Scotus points to a parallel between intellect and vision. The field of vision forms a conical pyramid from the eye. At the base of the cone are many things which are seen with decreasing degrees of distinctness. The object seen most distinctly is the one on which the axis of the pyramid falls. This is the situation according to nature, but by an exercise of will that situation can change, for without moving our eye, and without any change in the position of the objects within the field of vision we can, by an act of will, focus our attention elsewhere than upon the object upon which the axis of the pyramid falls, and as a result we see a peripheral object more distinctly than we had done.

It is Scotus's contention that objects of intellect stand in much the same relation to will as do objects of vision. He asks: *Quomodo voluntas regit intellectum?* – 'In what way does will govern intellect?', and begins his reply by noting that for any perfect and distinct object of an act of intellect there can be many indistinct and imperfect ones – exactly as with visual acts. Amongst the objects not at the point of focus of intellect there may be one which pleases will in some way. Will may also take pleasure in the very act of intellect of which that is the object. And this pleasure that will takes in the object or in the act can lead to the object being strengthened and intensified. It is common experience that an idea at the edge of our thinking attracts our attention, as a result of which we proceed to investigate the idea more closely, and proceed to do so by an act of will. In that sense it is appropriate to speak of an act of intellect as the effect of an act of will. Hence though intellect is a cause of acts of will, it does not follow that intellect has primacy, for it could be argued that since will is the cause of acts of intellect, will must have primacy. I conclude that if causal efficacy is a proof of primacy then intellect and will each have primacy over the other, which seems absurd. It follows, in line with Scotus's own words, that causal antecedence is not a proof of primacy.

However, in light of the slogan *Nihil volitum quin praecognitum,* a doubt may yet be raised against Scotus's doctrine that will has primacy. Let us grant that will cannot do anything except in the light of a prior act of intellect. Intellect on the other hand can certainly act without a prior act of will. It seems to follows that the two powers, of will and intellect, are not after all on the same level, for will is dependent upon intellect, and intellect is not dependent upon will. Since what is dependent cannot have primacy over what it depends on, it follows that will cannot have primacy over intellect. Scotus mentions this argument but is not impressed by it. The question at issue is whether what is dependent can have primacy over that upon which it depends.

Scotus offers as a counter example the relation between means and ends.[7] As regards a means–end relation, the end is of course dependent upon the means. If we cannot employ the means then their end will not be achieved. Yet it is plain that even though the end is dependent for its existence upon the means, within the means–end relation it is the end, rather than the means, that has primacy, for the means are for the sake of the end, and not vice versa. Hence the fact that something is dependent does not imply that it does not have primacy over what it is dependent on.

Scotus leaves it to us to recognise that even if in one respect the end is dependent upon the means, in two other respects the dependency relation goes in the opposite direction. First there is a dependency of existence. For if the means were adopted only in order to produce the end aimed at, then the means would not exist if it were not for the end. In that sense the existence of the means depends upon the existence of the end, and not vice versa. Secondly there is a dependency of value. For the value of the means depends upon the value of the end – something in which we find no value becomes vested by us with value when we see in the thing the possibility of using it as a means to an end that we seek to realise.

It is really the primacy of value that Scotus has in mind when discussing the primacy of will. Here again we meet the idea that love of God has greater value than has knowledge of Him. Yet love is located in will as knowledge is located in intellect. On that basis, the conclusion Scotus draws, that will has primacy, is irresistible.

Nothing is more basic to Scotus's system than the doctrine of the freedom of will. Yet the question whether will is free was a topic of intense debate in the Middle Ages. The chief grounds for doubting our freedom were thought to be provided by the doctrines of divine prescience and human predestination. These doctrines jointly appear to imply that what we do and what our state will be are matters not in our hands, but in God's. In Lecture Four I shall investigate this line of attack on the doctrine of free will, and shall base my discussion on the writings of a fifteenth-century Scottish philosopher who demonstrably worked in the shadow of Scotus.

NOTES

1. T. F. Torrance, *The Hermeneutics of John Calvin.*
2. See *Duns Scotus on the Will and Morality*, Selected and translated with an Introduction by Allan B. Wolter, O.F.M., pp. 268–87. The passage is Ordinatio III, suppl. dist. 37.
3. Aquinas, *Summa Theologiae* 1a2ae, 17, 1 ad 2.
4. '... volitio est effectus posterior intellectione naturaliter, et intellectio phantasmate vel phantasiatione, et propter illum ordinem necessarium, non potest causari volitio a voluntate, nisi prius causetur ab intellectu intellectio.' *Opus Oxoniense*, II, d. 25, quaestio unica, n. 19, in Scotus, *Opera Omnia*, ed. Wadding, vol. XIII, p. 212b.
5. Scotus first uses the phrase in the course of an argument to the effect that the will is necessitated: 'Impressio facta ab objecto in voluntate est pondus, et inclinatio; sed omne pondus inclinans necessitat inclinatum suum, nisi inclinatum renitatur, sed non renitatur, nisi per actum, etc.' *Collationes* XVI, n. 3, in Scotus, *Opera Omnia*, ed. Wadding, vol. V, p. 209b. But he rejects the argument: 'sed impressum in voluntate est tantum inclinans, ideo voluntas nunquam necessitatur ab obiecto', *ibid.*, p. 210b.
6. 'Difficile est voluntatem non inclinari ad id, quod est dictatum a ratione practica ultimatim, non tamen est impossibile.' *Reportata Parisiensia* II, d. 39, q. 2, n. 5, in Scotus, *Opera Omnia*, ed. Wadding, vol. XXIII, p. 205a. Scotus is here contrasting free will with practical reason. The passage just quoted is preceded by the assertion: 'intellectus practicus est, qui necessario assentit agibilibus, voluntas autem libere.'
7. *Opus Oxoniense*, IV, d. 49, q. ex lat., n. 189, in Scotus, *Opera Omnia*, ed. Wadding, vol. XXI, p. 155.

Lecture 4

Divine knowledge and human freedom

THE QUESTION of the nature of the link between divine knowledge and human freedom is systematically related to the topic which chiefly concerned us in Lectures Two and Three, namely Duns Scotus's account of the mental faculties of intellect and will. I shall start my discussion in this lecture by justifying the claim that these various topics are indeed systematically related, and thereafter I shall focus upon a line of attack on Scotus's teaching on free will.

We observed that Scotus held there to be an indivisible unity of the faculties of intellect and will in the human mind. The being of each is the same as the being of the other. This doctrine prompts the question why we speak of two faculties, when mind is an indivisible unity. Scotus's answer is that we start from the observation that there are at least two radically different sorts of mental act, understanding and willing, and we draw the conclusion that two such different sorts of act must be referred to different principles of action in the mind. We call one principle the faculty of intellect, that by which we understand, and we call the other the faculty of will.

This move would be resisted by a member of the Ockhamist Tendency. His chosen weapon would be a Razor. With the help of it he would seek to persuade us that for a faculty of intellect to exist is nothing more than for mind to be able to understand, and for a faculty of will to exist is nothing more than for mind to be able to will. He could point out that the doctrine of the unity of mind is not jeopardised by this account of the mode of existence of mental faculties for it is the very same mind that is able to perform these different sorts of act.

But Scotus, unlike some later Scottish philosophers, did not follow that path. While denying that mind has distinct parts, its various faculties, he believed there to be a basis in reality for distinguishing between intellect and will, a basis that does not consist simply of the difference between the different sorts of act. The distinction between the two faculties cannot just be the mind's being able to perform distinct sorts of act, for there must be something about mind that makes it possible for it to behave in this differentiated way. Scotus's solution, as we recall, is that mind, a unitary being, takes distinct forms, or, in his terminology, distinct 'formalities'. Just as acts of mind take different forms, such as the form of willing, of understanding, of imagining, and of remembering, so also mind itself takes various forms, of a willer, of an understander, of an imaginer, and a recollecter.

It follows that there is more to our faculty of will than just our acts of willing, for there is also that feature of mind in virtue of which we can will, namely, a particular sort of form or formality that mind takes. We identify any particular formality of mind, say the formality of will, in terms of acts of a distinctive form. The acts that mind performs in virtue of having that formality are acts of willing. As regards what it is about will in virtue of which we say it acts freely, Scotus's answer, we may recall, is that it is will's ability to produce contrary effects, so that in the very circumstance in which it produces a given effect it could produce a contrary one. It is not that it can produce both those contrary effects simultaneously, but rather that simultaneously it could equally produce either of them.

If there is no such thing as a human free will, as thus defined, then Scotus's philosophy of mind is mistaken at its core. Is Scotus mistaken in affirming that we have a free will? The question whether we have one is debated in modern times on the basis of a common perception regarding the universality of natural law. If all matter is governed by causal law then how can there be room for any free act by material beings? The question whether we have a free will was no less a topic of debate in the Middle Ages also, except that the chief obstacle to the affirmation of freedom was then perceived to come not from the realm of natural science but from that of theology. In brief, how can human freedom be compatible with predestination and divine prescience? These two theological doctrines jointly appear to imply that what we do, and what our state will be, are matters not in our hands, but in God's.

Duns Scotus discusses this topic in his *Commentary on the Sentences of Peter Lombard*, and it is a topic that Lombard himself deals with at the end of his *Sentences*, Book I. We shall see in Lectures Five and Six that the assent of faith, saying 'yes' as an act of faith, is essentially a free act. To argue against the freedom of our will is therefore by implication to argue against the possibility of faith. It is clearly important to deal with this most serious of the lines of attack mounted in the Middle Ages against the existence of human free will. Now that I have completed my examination of Scotus's concept of a free will, and am about to enter into an examination of the concept of the free assent of faith as developed by late-medieval Scottish philosophers, it is appropriate to pause to consider the central theological argument of the late-medieval period against free will, and to consider the response to it made within the Scottish philosophical tradition.

The late-medieval philosopher to whom I shall turn for help is John Ireland. When, in the second of his *magna opera*, he wrote in defence of the faith, he invoked the name and arguments of Duns Scotus, whom he refers to as 'Doctor Subtilis that was a great clerk of Paris and born of this land'.[1] He then tells us that 'the doctor subtle in his *Book of the Sentences* in the Prologue induces eight manner of ways to prove and persuade the faith'. The eight ways are thereupon reported and developed. Scotus is again invoked in Ireland's discussion of the relation between freedom and divine prescience.[2] In turning to John Ireland, therefore, we are not moving from the shadow of the Subtle Doctor.

Ireland's most substantial work of theology was his commentary on the *Sentences of Peter Lombard*. Only the second half of that huge commentary survives, the sole extant manuscript being in the library of the University of Aberdeen. The preparation of a critical edition, or at least of a good working edition, of that manuscript would be an invaluable contribution to the study of Pre-Reformation Scottish culture.

Another important source for his theological ideas is his *Mirror of Wisdom*, written in Scots for King James IV. It was from the *Mirror of Wisdom* that I took Ireland's remarks concerning Scotus that I cited earlier. The book was intended, at least in part, as a piece of advice concerning the duties of kingship – a literary exercise fraught with obvious dangers, though Ireland, who had been confessor to James III, had the tact and discretion necessary for so risky an exercise as advising James III's son how to govern.

The appropriateness of a theological context for advice on governorship is based on the belief that God's governance of the universe, as described in Scripture, should serve as a model for the governance exercised by any earthly monarch. God established a perfect law for His creatures, and since He is also perfectly well-informed about us, He is able to reward and punish us exactly as justice requires. An earthly monarch must approximate as closely as possible to this model, first by legislating just laws, and secondly by having the fullest possible information about his subjects, for otherwise they may not receive their due recompense. The links between divine and earthly governance are plain. The key links are the perfection of the laws and the fulness of the ruler's knowledge. It is with the latter of these that I shall here be concerned.

Let us think about the role played by God's knowledge and, more precisely, about the implications that God's knowledge has for the free will or otherwise of His creatures. In Lecture Two I discussed the doctrine of intellectual determinism, the doctrine that intellect so constrains will that there is nothing that will can do except act in response to and in conformity with the directives of intellect. What I am probing now is a kind of intellectual determinism but on a universal scale, with God's knowledge constraining us absolutely so that it is impossible for us to perform acts other than those that God knew from all eternity we would perform. This is not precisely the same version of intellectual determinism as that discussed previously, for as regards that earlier version the agent's intellect was seen as determining his own acts of will, but in the theological case what is at issue is whether God's knowledge determines not the acts of His own will but the acts of every human will. Nevertheless there is an obvious similarity between these two cases. Each features the idea that an act of intellect determines an act of will, thereby leaving no room for a free exercise of will.

Ireland accepts the default position, that we human beings have a free will, and he investigates its implications for God's power. We are free to sin, but would it not have been better if, instead of punishing us for sinning, God had so arranged things that though free we would not sin? Is it that God did not have the power to do this? Ireland's answer is 'no'. He believed that among creatures there are angels and those in a state of beatitude, who are free but who by God's grace do not sin. The concept of free will that Ireland appears to have in mind is that developed by Duns Scotus, according to whom to be free is simultaneously to be able to produce opposite effects. Freedom to keep God's law implies freedom to infringe that law. The possibility of sinning is therefore the price we pay for our freedom, just as unfreedom is a price other beings pay for the impossibility of their sinning.

Some might say that we pay a high price, but the question is whether it is unjustifiably high. Ireland's reason for thinking that it is not is a form of the so-called 'free will defence'. If God had created us without a free will the world would have been, in Ireland's word, 'imperfect'. Freedom is a great dignity in the world, sufficient to outweigh the value of human sinlessness. The metaphysical basis of the dignity of our freedom is the status of the human free will as *imago dei voluntatis*. God by an act of will created other beings, us, who also have a will. It is in this sense that we are said to be in the image and likeness of God.[3] Ireland is explicit on this. It is not in virtue of our intellect but of our will that we have this relation to God. There are overtones here of Scotus's doctrine of the primacy of will over intellect and the related doctrine of the primacy of love over knowledge, for love resides in and is the highest exercise of the will, whereas knowledge resides in the lesser faculty, the intellect.

It is not clear how we should weigh the relative merits of free will and sinlessness, both of which characterise God; though we might suspect that John Ireland's first step towards weighing them was to note that God created us with the freedom to sin. For if the good God created us with such a nature, this implies that it is better that we be capable of sinning than that we not exist at all.

The fact that we freely sin is deployed by Ireland as the basis for a moral argument for the existence of God. The shape of the argument is this: reason and justice demand that we be recompensed according to our deeds. Other human beings cannot recompense us with any assurance of judging recompense aright, and creatures below us cannot do this either. There must therefore be 'ane aboue the man'[4] whose task this is. The argument is neatly summed up by Ireland as: '*Homo potest peccare, ergo Deus est*' – 'A human being can sin, therefore God exists.'[5]

Sin is a crime against the universe, for with sin 'all the world would be broken in the perfection of it'.[6] Sin produces therefore what would be a vacuum if God did not intervene. The vacuum in question is of course moral, not physical, and it can be filled by divine acts of justice whereby recompense is bestowed exactly according to deserts. In this context Ireland refers to Aristotle's disproof of the possibility of a physical vacuum. It is Ireland's view that there can no more be a moral vacuum than a physical one, where a moral vacuum is emptiness produced by an act for which the agent does not receive due recompense. Thus it is the failure of the universe to respond appropriately to sin that would be accounted a moral vacuum.

From John Ireland's perspective therefore the universe has a moral structure, in the sense that it is governed in accordance with principles of justice. There cannot be free agents without there being justice, for their virtues and vices attract due recompense. I cannot speak about recompense in this context without reference to hell, a central feature of John Ireland's world-view, though not of mine. Nowadays we do not find theologians, or philosophers, with much to say about hell. It may yet make a comeback on the agenda of theologians, but during the Middle Ages it was very much on the agenda.

Perhaps it should be added, out of respect for Lord Gifford's project, that at least from the perspective of a John Ireland it is appropriate to speak about hell under the general heading of natural theology. Ireland regarded the existence of hell as almost a postulate of practical reason, answering to the perceived need for punishment commensurate with wickedness. His sense of natural justice told him as much, and we should therefore not be too shy nor too embarrassed to speak about hell.

John Ireland was not too shy or too embarrassed. His conclusion, unexpected though logically well founded, is that it is wrong to conceive of hell as a perfectly bad place. Far from it. On the basis of a crucial principle of assessment it is as good as heaven. Hell is a just place, for it and heaven are pre-eminently the places where divine justice is done. In one sense hell is a more just place than heaven, for there are those in heaven, we are told, who are there by an act of divine mercy, not of justice. Indeed it appears to be Ireland's doctrine that all human beings who are in heaven are there by an act of divine mercy rather than justice. For Ireland dwells on the fact that 'life and glory eternal are supernatural that exceed without proportion our fragility', and concludes: 'Therefore there is no human creature that by virtue of his proper nature may perform any work or operation meritorious of glory, joy and life eternal, but for that is required a gift of God and supernatural virtue that is called grace.'[7] The contrast Ireland sees between heaven and hell is articulated in a phrase chilling in its enthusiasm: 'His noble justice shines in hell in the punishment of the damned person, as His high and noble mercy in heaven.'[8] Hell is a just place not because people behave justly there, but because God performs there His justly punitive acts.

John Ireland's position might seem contradictory. On the one hand hell is the worst possible place in the world, and on the other Ireland sees it also as matching heaven in its virtuousness. But there is no contradiction. For the reprobate sinner hell must indeed seem the worst possible place for it is where he suffers the worst possible punishment, though, in accordance with a logical move made famous by Plato,[9] the sinner should be grateful for the opportunity to endure a penal sentence whose severity prevents the world being imperfect. There is therefore, after all, something nice to say about hell.

Indeed it might even seem that hell is a better place than our world, the one we inhabit on our pilgrims' way, for people sin here yet do not necessarily receive here their divine recompense. There thus appears to be a moral vacuum in this world while people await what is their due, and in that sense this is a world of injustice, unlike hell where every person receives his full measure. But John Ireland would not accept this description. His is a more spacious perspective; we should attend to the totality, not to the parts separately. The punishments of hell would not be just were it not for the sins committed in this life. The justice lies not in this world alone nor in the next alone, but in the total situation of pain inflicted as due recompense for a free act performed against God's law.

We have now seen sufficient of the theological context within which Ireland sets up his problem concerning human free will. He expounds the problem in these terms: God has 'infinite knowledge, wisdom, and all perfection',[10] and we must therefore ask 'why He should punish people so greatly, considering that His knowledge is so great and immutable that men may not make it false nor change it by any manner of means. And thus they say that whatever a man does he shall be condemned since God has knowledge of it, and they say that it does not profit man to do good or evil.'

There we have it. God's knowledge cannot be falsified nor changed by any manner of means, and hence we shall do precisely what He knew we would. If it was always going to be the case that we would do what God knew we would, then our supposedly free agency is entirely circumscribed by God's knowledge. It is as if our acts are products not of our free will but of God's knowledge, from which it would follow that God, not ourselves, must be accounted the agent of the acts in question. In so far as it is God's knowledge, the content of His intellect, that determines us to do what we do, the doctrine Ireland sets out to attack may appropriately be described as a form of intellectual determinism. That doctrine has an immediate moral implication, for if intellectual determinism, in any of its forms, is correct, then wherein lies the justice of the divine punishments meted out to us in virtue of our sinful acts? Surely the punishment is just only if we sin freely. And according to the doctrine of divine intellectual determinism we do not do anything freely, nor therefore sin freely.

Ireland characterises this argument as the product of a 'false and evil imagination'. Nevertheless he recognises that though fatally flawed it has some plausibility, and since it is false and also has a tendency to subvert morality it has to be met head on. He therefore replies in detail.

He is guided by the doctrine that God acts freely, a doctrine for which he provides a kind of cosmological proof. If the world were created by a necessary act, an act that God could not have prevented even had He wished to prevent it, then the world would exist necessarily. The world and everything in it would be eternal and, as Ireland puts the point: 'God might then in no way leave them unproduced nor might he destroy them.'[11] But on the contrary we see things come to be and cease to be. Things in the natural order have contingent, not necessary, existence, and that point, based upon common experience, is sufficient to undermine the claim that the world exists necessarily.

Yet God has knowledge or foreknowledge of everything that will be. And if He knows that they will be then necessarily they will be, and in that case when they exist they will exist necessarily and not contingently. But it has just been argued that since God acts freely all products of his acts are contingent and not necessary. What has gone wrong? Guided by Aquinas on this matter, Ireland argues that we have to be more careful about our use of the word 'necessary', and in particular we have to be clear about what is being said to be necessary when we argue that if God knows that a given event will occur then necessarily it will occur. In brief the necessity is not a feature of the event, nor even of the proposition that the event will occur. It is instead a feature of the logical relation between the two propositions (1) that God knows that the event will occur, and (2) that it will occur. What is necessary is this, that if God knows it will happen then it will happen. The event itself is contingent, for its occurrence is due in part to God's creative act, which was a free act. The contingent event might itself be a freely performed human act, and the fact that God knew from all eternity that it would be performed does not, according to the argument Ireland develops, contradict in any way the claim that the act is free.

There are propositions about the future of whose truth we are certain, such as that the mean temperature in Aberdeen in June will be higher (just) than the mean temperature in December, that there will be a full moon next week, and that there will be a high tide tomorrow in Aberdeen harbour at 7.16 pm. There are natural laws covering such facts, and our knowledge of those laws gives rise to our certainty that given events will occur. Whoever regards God's knowledge of the future as a bit like ours, will be inclined to regard our actions as determined, because an obvious explanation for the fact that God knows what will happen is that He knows the laws from which, with suitable other data, the future course of events can be inferred. However I know of no medieval philosopher who thought that this was a suitable model for understanding what God's knowledge of the future is like. Certainly John Ireland would have rejected it as an outlandish model, and would perhaps have given it the name 'anthroposcientism'.

In a key passage he writes: 'It is necessary that God who is the judge, the rewarder and punisher of all good and evil see and know at once all the works and deeds of word, heart, mind, intention, thought and cogitation of every man that is or was or ever shall be.'[12] God, then, knows the inner lives of us all, and knows them simultaneously. In a phrase to which Ireland makes explicit reference Boethius in the *Consolation of Philosophy* affirms that God 'looked out from the high turret (or "watch-tower") of providence'.[13] The picture is of God looking down upon human beings and seeing in a single, simple glance everything pass below Him. Boethius undoubtedly held that all events past, present, and future are simultaneously present to God. St Thomas Aquinas speaks in the same terms, and in doing so reflects Boethius's picture of God as looking down upon the created order, though Boethius speaks about God as in a high tower, and Aquinas's preferred metaphor is that of a person standing on top of a hill who is able to see simultaneously the travellers on the path which goes round the hill, even though the contours of the hill prevent each traveller from seeing those coming behind him. Thus does God, who is above the created world, see simultaneously the events which are related to each other in the relation of temporal before and after.[14]

That all events are simultaneously present to God has an implication drawn both by Aquinas and by John Ireland who seems to have had Aquinas's doctrine in mind, and who was certainly familiar with the *Prima Pars* of the *Summa Theologiae* in which Aquinas expounds it. I quote Ireland: 'When I see something, such as a man sit or stand, I am certain that he sits or stands. But my sight neither puts nor causes necessity in him. Likewise with the spiritual eye and sight of God. Though He sees this evil person fall into sin and persevere therein, and finally be condemned, yet God's knowledge is not the cause why he falls into sin and perseveres in it.'[15] Ireland's point, or at least an important part of it, is clear. Our acts, future to us, are present to the divine gaze, and so of course God knows that they will happen. But what he knows with certainty will happen are free acts. That I am certain of the occurrence of a human act does not imply that the act is not free. My certainty of it is due to the fact that I am now watching it unfold before me. Likewise if we suppose that all acts future to us are present to God, in the same timeless instant in which all acts past and present to us are present to God, then the fact that God knows with certainty what we shall do does not imply that those acts, when we get round to performing them, are not freely performed. Hence God's so-called 'foreknowledge' is not foreknowledge at all even though it includes knowledge of events which are future in relation to us now. Instead it is knowledge of what is immediately present to the knower. That is, God's knowing and the object known are simultaneous.

There does not purport to be in this a proof that human acts are free. There purports to be at most a criticism of one argument to the effect that our acts are not free, the argument criticised being that God knew from all eternity that our acts would be performed and hence if we do not perform them we would thereby falsify God's knowledge. His knowledge cannot be falsified, and therefore we are absolutely constrained to perform the acts God knew we would perform. The criticism is simply that our present knowledge of the occurrence of a human act unfolding before us does not imply that the act is not free, and by the same token God's knowledge of a human act unfolding before Him does not imply that it is not free. The difference between the two cases is that we do not know of the occurrence of human acts lying in the future in relation to us now, whereas nothing lies in the future in relation to God.

The problem I have just been discussing was a major battlefield in medieval theology. George Lokert and William Manderston, two leading Scottish theologians in the generation following Ireland, wrote treatises devoted to the topic.[16] John Mair also contributed to the discussion. For the remainder of this lecture I shall attend to the concept, central to the topic at issue, of a gaze which takes in simultaneously past, present and future events. This concept has generated a considerable literature, and my excuse for adding to it is that the concept has not before been discussed with specific reference to John Ireland. I shall begin by commenting briefly on the concept of simultaneity at issue.

When we see temporally successive events we see them successively. It is not merely that the events themselves are temporally successive, but that the seeing is also, in that either there is a single visual act which has successive parts, even if parts that are continuous with each other, or there are successive visual acts. According to Boethius and Aquinas a basic element in the concept of cognition *sub specie aeternitatis* is precisely that even where temporally successive events are seen, they are seen simultaneously. Of course we ask: If one thing is before another, how can the two be seen simultaneously? Is there a model that enables us to understand this concept? We all know what it is like to have the kind of privileged perspective possessed by the person in a watch-tower or on top of a hill. Boethius and Aquinas tell us that seeing the world *sub specie aeternitatis* is a bit like seeing from such a vantage point. If so, then we can indeed form the theological concept at issue.

But how helpful are these metaphors? Some, for example Anthony Kenny,[17] have pronounced them of no help whatever, on the grounds that the concept of simultaneity they were designed to elucidate is incoherent, as is proved by the fact that on the basis of that concept a contradiction can be generated. The generation of the contradiction is easily accomplished. If all events that occur throughout history are simultaneously present to the divine gaze, then the birth of Duns Scotus and the birth of David Hume are simultaneously present to it. Since they are simultaneous with the same thing those two births were simultaneous with each other. Yet they occurred four centuries apart and therefore were not simultaneous with each other. And that contradiction surely reveals the incoherence of the concept of simultaneity employed by theologians who hold that all events in history are simultaneously present to God's gaze.

Nevertheless I am not yet prepared to abandon hope that a persuasive account of the concept, an account establishing its coherence, can be given. I have to say that I have not myself found the metaphors of Boethius and Aquinas helpful. In particular, as regards Aquinas's mountaineering metaphor, whatever its other defects it trades too heavily upon the verbal identity of spatial and temporal idioms. X can be before Y or after Y in a temporal sense and in a spatial one. In Aquinas's model, though one traveller is walking before another spatially, he is not walking before the other temporally, for the man on top of the hill sees them simultaneously and *therefore* they are walking simultaneously. This does not help me to understand how two things which do not happen simultaneously can be seen simultaneously. I shall now work towards what I find a more illuminating metaphor.

A proposition that I utter takes time to come into existence in its entirety. Yet it is, or is likely to be, expressive of a thought that I am having, and it is not nearly so clear that my thought need take time in coming into existence in its entirety. What I say when I express my thought that Glasgow Cathedral is a beautiful building takes time to say. But the thought was present in my mind in its entirety from the moment when it was in my mind at all. There was no temporal order of construction, if indeed the thought has parts from which it can be supposed to have been constructed.

Whether a thought, that is, an act of thinking (*actus intelligendi*) has parts or not was the subject of debate in the Middle Ages. Gregory of Rimini, whom John Ireland invokes in the course of his discussion of divine foreknowledge and human free will, held that in itself a thought does not have parts. It has them only in the sense that the utterance which expresses the thought has them, or in the sense that what the thought is about has them.[18] But since the thought does not in itself have parts, the thought cannot be constructed out of parts – and this point is the basis of the possibility of the thought's being present in its entirety in the mind the moment any of it is.

In fact Gregory's was a minority report in the Middle Ages. Most philosophers followed William Ockham in holding that a propositional thought does indeed have parts, corresponding roughly to the parts of the spoken proposition.[19] But even so, the fact that the propositional thought has parts does not by itself imply that it has, or at any rate must have, a temporal order of construction. And here we cannot ignore the fact of experience, which I think is a fact, that sometimes we see something 'in a flash' or 'all at once', where we are completely unaware of any temporal ordering that the construction process might have. We are, then, sufficiently familiar with the experience of having a thought which did not come to us in any perceptible extension of time. And yet the spoken expression of that thought takes time where the whole significative element in the utterance is also in the thought. Is God's instantaneous grasp of the temporal world to be understood on the model of our instantaneous grasp of the sense of a proposition whose utterance takes time?

It might be claimed that the reason it is possible to have a thought instantaneously is precisely that a thought does not have a temporal structure. And it may be argued that since the world does have such a structure the fact that we know what it is to have a thought instantaneously gives us no insight into God's instantaneous knowledge of the world.

But there are thoughts and thoughts. Two kinds of case in particular seem to me worthy of close consideration. The first is poetry. There are cases of a poem suddenly occurring to a poet. A poem has to be read with due attention paid to its tempo, especially to the changes in speed, and it seems to me at least probable that the concept of the poem as an auditory experience is part of the overall concept of the poem that comes to the poet in an instant.

For our purposes this kind of example is particularly relevant because we are now dealing with an object, a poem, which is intrinsically temporal. Even in the very instant in which the poem occurs to the poet it possesses its own temporal structure.

I see no reason to reject the possibility of a poem occurring to a poet in an instant. And it is surely obvious that the complex temporal structure of a poem has a semantic function within that context. Change the temporal structure and you risk changing the meaning. I am not of course suggesting that all poetic composition is like that. Of course a poet might spend a month composing the poem, phrase by phrase, if not word by word. I am speaking only about what can happen when the fortunate poet, blessed by the muse, is presented with the completed work in its graceful, bewitching integrity all in an instant. The muse presents the work and suddenly the poet has it all when the moment before he had none of it.

I shall turn now to what I believe to be the best kind of example, that of musical composition. Musical concepts occur to composers as poetical ones occur to poets. I do not know sufficiently what Mozart had in mind when he remarked that a symphony had occurred to him, and neither do I know enough about the famous occasion on which Schubert, in the midst of a conversation with friends in a café, suddenly took the menu and wrote the score to *Ständchen*. But in any case no-one supposes that it takes the same time to have a musical idea and to give a performance of that same piece of music.

There are two points here. First, it was said of Beethoven that he could run his eye down a musical score and know just what the music sounded like. There was no question of his reading the music at the speed at which he would give a public performance of it. Perhaps in the space of a few seconds any gifted score-reader could grasp as much of the music as he could by listening to a much longer public performance given at the 'correct' speed, where by 'correct' I mean of course 'correct for a public performance'. Who is to say how fast an inner performance needs to be for it to be correct? As Thomas Hobbes remarks in a different context: 'For thought is quick.' The unfolding of the inner life of the spirit cannot to be measured by clocks which mark the passage of physical time.

Secondly, I wish to maintain that a musical idea can be presented by the muse, handed over in its entirety, in such a way that the composer does not have any part of it until he has it all. Nevertheless, in such a case the temporal structure is intrinsic to the musical idea, just as the temporal structure is intrinsic to the poem.

I have mentioned three musical geniuses, but in this kind of case it is not necessary to attend only to what geniuses do. Any composer must have the experience of getting ideas in an instant, even if they are not very good ideas. It is the fact that they are conceived in their entirety, the fact that they are immediately present from first note to last, which is important here, and not the aesthetic quality. In such an idea sustained in the mind of the composer the end truly is in the beginning.

I have deliberately taken as my example the poet and composer rather than the person to whom there occurs a poem or a musical composition by someone else. It is true that a line of Hopkins or a phrase of Mozart can come to mind in an instant. But I wish to include in my model something corresponding to *scientia approbationis*. Aquinas affirms that God's knowledge is the cause of what is known in so far as that knowledge is combined with will.[20] God's knowledge may, then, be compared with the knowledge that an artificer has of the things that he makes. Of course we cannot in this life know the extent to which the sudden inspiration of the poet or composer is an adequate model for the gaze which is *sub specie aeternitatis*. But I do think that this model is more helpful than Boethius's watchman in a high tower or Aquinas's mountaineer in providing us with some conception of how God can simultaneously perceive things that are temporally successive – He does so in somewhat the same way that the poet holds in his mind simultaneously the temporally structured poem with which he has suddenly been presented by the muse.

Here, then, we have a means to understanding John Ireland's claim that the world throughout its history is simultaneously present to God. The way is therefore open to argue, as Ireland does, that the fact that the world is present to God no more necessitates the events which God sees than the fact that given events are present to us necessitates the occurrence of those events. We recall that Ireland asks 'why [God] should punish people so greatly, considering that His knowledge is so great and immutable that men may not make it false nor change it by any manner of means. And thus they say that whatever a man does he shall be condemned since God has knowledge of it, and they say that it does not profit man to do good or evil.' Ireland is able to reply that though God knows the free acts of human beings and has known them from all eternity, those acts are not any the less free on account of God's knowledge of them. And if they are free and if they infringe the laws promulgated by the Lord of the universe, then in accordance with principles of wise governance, no injustice is perpetrated if God punishes the lawbreakers.

Scotus had made the concept of free will central to his philosophy of mind. The gravest attack on that concept came, as we have seen, from the direction of theology. We have now observed the defence mounted by John Ireland in an attempt to neutralise the attack. In relation to the subject matter of this series of lectures, the significance of Ireland's defence of the doctrine of human free will lies in the fact that the will is inextricably linked with the assent of faith. The relation between faith and will is the topic of Lecture Five.

NOTES

1. F. Quinn (ed.), *The Meroure of Wyssdome by Johannes de Irlandia,* vol. II, p. 106. I have modernised Ireland's spelling here and elsewhere in the chapter.
2. *Ibid.,* p. 147.
3. *Ibid.,* p. 115.
4. *Ibid.,* p. 119.
5. *Ibid.,* p. 121.
6. *Ibid.,* p. 119.
7. *Ibid.,* p. 130.
8. *Ibid.,* p. 150.
9. *Gorgias,* 480a–d.
10. *Meroure,* vol. II, p. 135.
11. *Ibid.,* p. 136.
12. *Ibid.,* p. 121.
13. Boethius, *Consolation of Philosophy* Loeb Classical Library, London 1968, IV, VI, lines 121–2 'qui . . . ex alta providentiae specula respexit'.
14. 'Unde nobis, quia cognoscimus futura contingentia ut talia sunt, certa esse non possunt: sed soli Deo, cuius intelligere est in aeternitate supra tempus. Sicut ille qui vadit per viam non videt eos qui post eum veniunt; sed ille qui ab aliqua altitudine totam viam intuetur, simul videt omnes transeuntes per viam' Aquinas, *Summa Theologiae* 1, 14, 13 ad 3.
15. *Meroure,* vol. II, p. 143.

16. William Manderston, *Tractatus de futuro contingenti*; George Lokert, *Questio subtillissima de futuro contingenti*.
17. A. Kenny, 'Divine foreknowledge and human freedom', in A. Kenny (ed.), *Aquinas: A Collection of Critical Essays*, pp. 255–70, see esp. p. 264.
18. Gregory of Rimini, *Super Primum et Secundum Sententiarum*, lib. 1, prol.q. 1, art. 3.
19. William Ockham, *Summa Logicae* Pars I, cap. 3, P. Boehner, G. Gál, S. Brown (eds), pp. 11–14.
20. 'Unde necesse est quod sua scientia sit causa rerum secundum quod habet voluntatem coniunctam' Aquinas, *Summa Theologiae* 1, 14, 8c.

Lecture 5

The nature of faith

IN THE past three lectures I have focused upon the concept of free will. In Lectures Two and Three I examined Duns Scotus's exposition of the concept. Then I turned to John Ireland, a Scottish theologian demonstrably working in the shadow of Scotus, and considered his defence of the claim that we do indeed have free will. Among the acts commonly thought of throughout the Middle Ages as exercises of free will are assents of faith, saying 'yes' as an act of faith, and I shall turn now to an examination of such assents. My main task here is the presentation of a definition of 'assent of faith'. The earlier discussions on Duns Scotus's account of intellect and will have an immediate implication for the assent of faith, for, as we shall see, such an assent involves two mental acts. The first is an act of intellect by which a probable argument is constructed and hesitant assent given to the conclusion purely as an act of intellect. And the second mental act is an act of will by which the assent to the conclusion, which had been given hesitantly, comes to be given firmly or without hesitation. As regards the definition of 'assent of faith' that I shall present, it will have a form recommended, and generally employed, by medieval philosophers, and the definition itself is the one generally accepted within the circle of John Mair.

As regards its form, it has two parts, the first indicating the genus of which faith is one species, and the second indicating the features which distinguish faith from the other species in that same genus. The genus in question is assent, saying 'yes'. To have faith that a given proposition is true is one, but only one, way of saying 'yes', and we learn a great deal about faith by seeing what other ways there are. In the part of my discussion dealing with the species of assent with which faith can be contrasted I shall attend to two species prominent in late-medieval discussions. The first is *evidentia*, or 'evident assent', and the second,

69

opinion or 'opinative assent'. As we shall see, there is a perspective from which these two sorts of mental act appear as the extremes between which the assent of faith lies. I shall start therefore by saying what faith is not, focusing in particular upon the fact that it is neither evident assent nor opinion. Thus my approach to faith takes me along the Via Negativa, the most famous methodological road tramped by theologians, and my purpose in taking this route is to clarify the concept of faith by displaying its location within the complex conceptual network which is its true home.

I have been assuming that all forms of assent are alike in their dependence upon the assenter's antecedent grasp of the sense of a proposition. Assent is, after all, to a proposition, and there must therefore be a proposition in place in the assenter's mind to which he can give assent. This is at least according to the natural course of things. Some philosophers, George Lokert of Ayr being one, wonder whether absolutely speaking there need be a proposition. Lokert invokes the important theological principle: if two things are really distinct, then God could annihilate either while preserving the other. But saying 'yes' to a proposition is really distinct from the proposition to which the assent is given and hence, according to the theological principle I have just enunciated, God could annihilate the proposition while preserving the assent. That, at any rate, is the thesis that Lokert presents for discussion.[1]

This is, however, a hard thesis to accept. Must we allow the possibility that a person can assent where there is not something to which he assents? The answer is surely 'no'. My argument against the thesis is that to assent without there being a proposition that is the object of the assent, is to assent to nothing, and to assent to nothing is not to assent at all. What, though, of the theological principle Lokert employed to reach his hard conclusion? I think that the principle, that of two really distinct things God can annihilate either while preserving the other, is inappropriately applied by Lokert to the particular case of an assent and the proposition to which assent is given. For the two are not really distinct. There is a single act of assenting to a proposition, and the assenting and the proposition are related in the act as form to content. The fact that we can make a distinction in our intellect between the assenting and the proposition does not in the least imply that the two can exist distinct from each other in reality as well as in the intellect.

The situation is comparable with our ability to distinguish between, say, the sphericity of a sphere and the content of that same sphere.

That we can make that distinction in our intellect does not in the least imply that there can exist in reality a sphericity which is not the sphericity of something. For sphericity to exist is for there to be something spherical. In the same way, for an assent to exist is for something to be assented to.

For the remainder of this lecture I shall assume that any act of assent, whether an assent of knowledge, of faith or of opinion, has a propositional content, and on that basis I shall proceed to a discussion of the principles separating these various forms of assent. An excellent starting point for this enquiry, as for much else in theology, is St Anselm's famous phrase '*fides quaerens intellectum*' – 'faith seeking understanding', the phrase which opened this series of lectures, and the phrase also which, better than any other, defines medieval philosophy. St Anselm's faith provided him with the objects which in a philosophical way he sought to understand. Most importantly he began with faith in God and he then held that faith up to the clear bright light of his intellect in order to understand as fully as possible who it was in whom he had faith. Hence for St Anselm intellect is no enemy of faith; it is on the contrary a means to its enrichment.

It is customary to interpret St Anselm as seeking to prove the existence of the God in whose existence he had previously only had faith. In so far as he provides a demonstration of God's existence he can thereafter claim to know that God exists, and not merely to have faith that He does. In short, if the customary interpretation of Anselm's *Proslogion* is correct then Anselm has, by the exercise of intellect alone, progressed from faith to knowledge.

But as I indicated in an earlier lecture, I believe this a mistaken account of St Anselm's project. There is strong reason to interpret him instead as seeking not to prove God's existence but, on the contrary, to give an account of its nature, a nature which is unlike that of the existence of any created thing. Starting with the concept of a being greater than which cannot be thought, Anselm demonstrates that such a being cannot not exist, as contrasted with every created thing, which has only contingent existence. The conclusion of the argument therefore, is that God has necessary existence. As Anselm also puts the point, God *truly* exists, by which he does not mean simply that God exists, but that he does not have the possibility of not existing. On this latter interpretation, therefore, St Anselm's acceptance on *faith* that God exists was not, after the successful completion of the demonstration in the *Proslogion*, replaced by *knowledge* of His existence. Far from advancing from faith to knowledge, he advanced from a less insightful to a more insightful faith, a faith which thereafter rested upon a deeper insight into the nature of the divine existence.

Neither do I think that after his discovery of the so-called ontological argument for God's existence St Anselm advanced from a lesser degree of certainty or sureness regarding God's existence to a greater degree. He never could have been surer of the existence of God than he was when, in the preamble to the alleged proof, he prayed to God for guidance. We are speaking here of a man as sure of God's existence as he was of his own.

(I add in parenthesis that perhaps I should not be using here the value-loaded term 'advance', speaking as I do of an advance from faith to knowledge. The interesting claim that knowledge is an advance on faith stands in need of proof, though I do not deny that the claim may be true.)

Be that as it may, it is clear that knowing that a given proposition is true and having faith that it is are not the same cognitive state. Perhaps indeed they are mutually exclusive. There is a complicated story to be told in support of this suggestion, and I shall shortly be providing that support, but for the moment we can notice the absurdity of a person claiming to accept on faith that a given object exists if the object is right in front of him and he is staring at it. I do not mean 'staring sightlessly' – something we can all do – but staring comprehendingly at the object. He knows the object exists, for there it is, right in front of him; he does not have faith that it exists. Likewise it is absurd for a person to claim faith in the truth of a proposition if he has a demonstrative proof of it. He knows it is true, and the demonstration leaves no room for faith.

What is the difference between faith and knowledge? It is plainly not a matter of degree of conviction or certainty. A person might be every bit as certain of the truth of a proposition he holds on faith as he ever could be of a proposition he knows to be true on the basis of utterly straightforward perceptual evidence. The difference lies elsewhere. The time has come to start to unpack the notion of assent of knowledge.

Such an assent was termed by the Pre-Reformation Scottish philosophers *evidentia*, a word for which there is no entirely satisfactory translation. The word 'evidence' is inadequate for the task, for a fact could be recognised as 'evidence' for a claim even though it produces much less than certainty or assuredness that the claim is true, whereas *evidentia* implies certainty. 'Evidentness' is a better translation, for at least if the truth of a proposition is evident to us then we are certain or sure that it is true.

But there is much more to *evidentia* than that. It is a technical term in Pre-Reformation philosophy and has to be treated on that basis. John Mair tells us that *evidentia* is '(1) an assent which is (2) true, (3) unhesitant, (4) caused by principles which necessitate the intellect, and (5) in thus assenting the intellect cannot be deceived'.[2] David Cranston gives a definition which, at least verbally, does not accord entirely with Mair's. He tells us that *evidentia* is '(1) an assent, which is (2) true, (3) naturally caused, (4) unhesitant, (5) whether or not the intellect, in thus assenting, can be deceived'.[3] The disagreement between the two definitions lies chiefly in the fact that Mair holds that the person giving evident assent cannot be deceived whereas Cranston speaks about a person being able to give such assent 'whether or not in thus assenting he can be deceived'.

In fact the disagreement here is verbal but not substantive. A distinction is made by both men between what happens according to the routine working out of natural processes, and what can happen by God's absolute power when He causes to happen an event that would not have occurred but for a special act of God. A distinction is also made between those assents whose content is of such a nature that not even God could cause us to be deceived when we make them, and those assents in which we could not be deceived except by a special act of God. When Mair affirms that in giving evident assent we cannot be deceived he has in mind assent in which we cannot be deceived in so far as God is not interfering with the ordinary course of nature. On the other hand when Cranston affirms that a given assent can be evident whether we are being deceived or not, he is acknowledging the fact that God can by a special act cause to happen something that would not have happened had nature taken its course.

Both men affirm that evident assent is *sine formidine*, that is, un-hesitant. Mair helps us to understand this deployment of the term 'unhesitant' by saying that its inclusion in the definition is intended to rule out suspicion, conjecture or opinion as possible forms of evident assent.[4] It is easy to see why conjecture and suspicion are excluded by the term 'unhesitant', but it seems odd to say that an assent cannot be given in the form of an opinion if it is unhesitant. The obvious point to make is that a person can hold an opinion with just the degree of assurance with which he assents to propositions whose truth he is able to demonstrate with impeccable logic. So why say, as Mair and Cranston do, that an opinion is an assent given hesitantly? The answer is that 'opinion' is being used as a technical term, and among the defining features it is declared to have is precisely the hesitation or lack of assurance with which the assent is given. And with it is contrasted evident assent.

What kinds of thing come under the heading 'evident assent'? The question is important, for through its answer we reach a clue regarding the nature of faith. My assent to the proposition that there is a sheet of white paper before me is an evident assent. So also is my assent to the proposition that I am seated at this desk. These are true propositions, and I give my assent with assurance. And the assent is naturally caused, in that I have merely to open my eyes and look, and I see the paper, and see the desk. The unhesitating assent to the propositions in question is something over which I exercise no voluntary control. Certainly my will is not involved. We are here quite close to the etymological root of the term 'evident'. There are some things that we *see* to be true, and especially we are naturally given to accepting the evidence of our own eyes. That is surely the securest sort of ground for assent. I know something happened because I saw it happen. Such assent is called natural evident assent.

But secure as it is, it is not the most secure possible. Here we must remember that discussions about assent took place within a theological context. God's power could not be ignored. Was there not after all the theoretical possibility that God might cause us to be deceived? George Lokert considers his assent to the proposition that the wall he is looking at is white. The wall is a substance with properties such as its colour, shape, texture, and so on. And Lokert sees the wall as a substance with these various properties. But might God not annihilate the substance of the wall while retaining in place those various properties? Surely He could, and if He has done so, then Lokert is after all not looking at a wall, for a wall is a substance with a certain form and God has annihilated the substance.[5]

Some features of this example are puzzling, but the crucial point for us is that Lokert and his colleagues recognised that our perceptual knowledge is not so securely based that we are absolutely secure from deception in giving assent on the basis of the plain evidence of our senses.

But what could be more secure than assent based upon the evidence of our own senses? Yet it was held that many things could. A century before Descartes John Mair and his colleagues took 'I exist' as their model of a proposition in giving assent to which we could not be deceived even by God's exercise of His absolute power. Assent to such a proposition was termed 'highest evident assent', which Gilbert Crab of Aberdeen defined thus: 'Highest evident assent is certain, naturally caused assent, through which, in assenting, the intellect cannot be deceived whether by a natural or a supernatural power.'[6]

Propositions that were classed as necessary truths also were regarded as fitting objects of highest evident assent. George Lokert states baldly: 'There is no necessary proposition which is given anything but absolute [i.e. highest] evident assent. Since a proposition is necessary it is impossible for a power to be deceived in assenting to it.'[7] On this view, in saying yes to 'A whole is greater than each of its parts' I cannot be deceived even by God. I can assent to the proposition that the wall I am looking at is white, and be in error because God has, so to say, tampered with the evidence. He has annihilated the substance of the wall while preserving the various qualities. But the proposition 'A whole is greater than each of its parts' is of such a nature that, however much God tampers with whatever evidence I might be relying on for my assent, I cannot be deceived in saying 'yes'. There is no pause. Having grasped the sense of the proposition, I give my assent unhesitantly and with absolute assurance that I am right.

In distinguishing between highest evident assent and natural evident assent, the Pre-Reformation Scottish philosophers did not focus on a distinction between degrees of unhesitancy. The distinction was made entirely on the basis of the fact that we can, absolutely speaking, be deceived in assenting to some propositions, and absolutely speaking cannot be deceived in assenting to others. I am, after all, just as unhesitant in assenting to the proposition that this sheet of paper is white as in assenting to the proposition that a whole is greater than each of its parts. But this matter is not entirely plain sailing, and I should like here to indicate the nature of the problem. The exposition will set the scene for the introduction of my discussion on faith. It is precisely in this context that my Scottish philosophers introduced their discussions of faith.

A naturally evident assent is one through which the assenter can be deceived by an act of God, though if nature runs its ordinary course, that is, without divine interference, the assenter is not deceived. We often give naturally evident assent. How do we manage it? One answer is that there is nothing we can do about it. There are original features of our nature upon which we rely by nature. One such is the trust we place in our senses. That is just us. We are dealing here with a process which is not subject to voluntary control. I cannot look at this sheet of paper and withhold my assent from the proposition that it is white.

The doctrine of naturally evident assent is not free of difficulty, and I should like here to speak briefly about the problem. I should emphasise that the problem I have in mind is not one which worried our late-medieval Scottish philosophers, but a version of it has worried philosophers ever since Descartes' discussion of it in his *Meditations*. The problem at issue arises from the fact that all the philosophers I have been discussing held that there are two aspects to God's power. First there is the ordinate power of God by which He works through nature, so that whatever happens in the ordinary course of nature happens in consequence of God's will, and secondly there is the absolute power of God by which He can produce an effect which would not occur if nature were left to run its ordinary course.

In the light of their acknowledgement of these two aspects to God's power – for they are not two powers but two aspects to the one power – our philosophers were surely logically well placed to draw the conclusion that their so-called naturally evident assent was not after all naturally caused, but was instead caused at least partially by an act of will. If I know that God by His absolute power is able to override nature and annihilate a substance while preserving the qualities, I must acknowledge the possibility that I am being deceived when I believe that this sheet of paper is white. In that case I am surely entitled to conclude that if I say 'yes' unhesitantly to the proposition that this sheet of paper is white I must be doing so partly by an act of will.

I might of course try to argue that since God is no deceiver He would not interfere with nature in such a way as to leave me in error as to what substances there are in the world. But I would still be committed to saying that my will contributed to my assent. For it is only by an act of will that I firmly assent to the premiss that God would not deceive me. And if that firm assent is by an act of will, then so also must be my firm assent to the conclusion that this sheet of paper is white, which I draw on the partial basis of that premiss.

Nevertheless our late-medieval philosophers were not attracted to this line of reasoning. They were convinced that there are indeed such acts as natural evident assents, and saw no reason to assign a role to the will in the production of assent to propositions affirming the existence of objects which are immediately present to their senses. Our philosophers seem to have taken the view that theological knowledge concerning God's absolute power to deceive a person who says 'yes' to such propositions, can have no practical effect on the assenter. Though he knows that God could deceive him, he remains utterly incapable of believing or opining that he actually is being deceived. For example, whatever my views about God's power, I cannot believe, while staring at this paper, that it is perhaps not white. With respect to such basic matters as the contents of the physical world in which we live, our late-medieval Scots did not have a belief system very different from that of all other mortals. Though there was available to them theological material upon which one could base a philosophy thoroughgoing in its scepticism, they made no attempt to develop such a thing.

There is a difference between grasping a proposition and judging whether it is true or not. And it is surely obvious that grasping a proposition is, in some sense of the term, antecedent to assenting to it – though perhaps we do not have to say that the antecedence is temporal, for there are propositions to which we say 'yes' as soon as we understand them. On such occasions understanding and assent seem to occur simultaneously. It does not follow of course that the assent is unstoppable. Granted parallel moves that he makes in other contexts, George Lokert is logically committed to holding that since grasping a proposition and saying 'yes' to it are different acts, it would be possible for God to preserve the first act, the apprehension, while preventing the occurrence of the second, the assent. Without doubt Lokert held that we are so constructed as to give unhesitant assent to certain propositions; the fact that we give such assent is an original feature of our nature. But God could have created us differently, and might yet interfere with the ordinary course of nature to produce in us on occasion an act contrary to the one that nature would produce if left to its own devices. Thus God could, by the exercise of his absolute power, cause us to dissent from the proposition 'A whole is greater than each one of its parts' after we had grasped the sense of the proposition. The point is that by the exercise of His ordinary power, His *potentia ordinata*, He causes us to give unhesitant assent to such propositions as soon as we grasp their sense.

Let us here continue to attend to the ordinary course of events. If evident assent is (1) true, (2) unhesitant, (3) naturally caused, and (4) of such a nature that the assenter cannot be deceived, then we might suppose that inevident assent is assent from which one of these four features is absent. Either it is untrue or it is hesitant or it is not naturally caused or it is an assent through which the the assenter can be deceived. It therefore comes as a surprise to read David Cranston's definition: 'Inevident assent is assent which is certain, without hesitation, and purely freely caused, for example, the assent to this: "God is three and one". It cannot be caused in the human intellect without a command of the will. And every such assent is called an assent of faith. So Augustine says on this matter: "No one can believe without willing".'[8]

But the term 'faith' is ambiguous, and Cranston is quick to elucidate. He writes: '"Faith" has two senses. In one sense it is an assent to a proposition which is formally or equivalently commanded in the law of God . . . In the second sense it is any assent which is freely caused by the authority of the speaker, whether or not it is commanded [by God].'[9] The first of these two senses – that faith is assent to a proposition commanded in God's law – is the narrower sense and is included in the second one – that it is assent freely caused by the authority of a speaker, whoever it may be. Cranston is here acknowledging that not all faith is religious faith, and his position on this matter seems unexceptionable. But there are grounds for puzzlement in the fact that he identifies the assent of faith as the only sort of inevident assent. There are surely many other sorts. One is the assent of opinion, which is like evident assent in being naturally caused, but is unlike evident assent in that it is given hesitantly and in giving it the assenter may be deceived.

I believe the explanation is that, of the three kinds of assent that our philosopher-theologians discussed, evident assent, assent of faith and finally opinative assent, it was the first two, evident assent and the assent of faith, that were regarded as of especial interest. The first of these, evident assent, is bound to interest the philosopher, and the second, faith, is bound to interest the theologian. The third, the assent of opinion, was of interest partly because consideration of it enables us to learn more about evident assent and faith by seeing what they can be contrasted with, and partly because opinative assent plays a crucial role in the assent of faith. As regards inevident assent, faith was much more a matter of professional interest to the philosopher-theologians of Mair's circle than was opinion. And for that reason they sometimes wrote, as David Cranston did, as if faith were the only kind of inevident assent. Nevertheless, for the reasons just given, opinative assent could not be ignored. In addition, as I indicated at the start of this lecture, from a given perspective faith lies on an axis between evident assent and opinion. I should like to explore this perspective here.

There are two distinctions to be drawn between evident assent and opinion. The first is that in giving evident assent we cannot be deceived, whereas we can be deceived in holding an opinion. The second is that evident assent is given without hesitation, whereas we opine only hesitantly. There was a commonly held view that the two sorts of assent differ not merely in degree but in kind or species. In that case the question of hesitation is not of primary importance in distinguishing between these two ways of saying 'yes', for there is a scale of hesitation on which total absence of hesitation is located as a terminus. Being more hesitant, less hesitant, and unhesitant, differ in degree rather than in species. Perhaps therefore in seeking to identify the crucial difference between the two ways of saying 'yes' it would be better to focus on the fact that in giving the one sort of assent we cannot be deceived and in giving the other we can.

George Lokert, who is very clear about the need to posit a specific difference between these ways of saying 'yes', draws the conclusion that 'therefore no evident assent can become inevident, or vice versa'.[10] Yet counter-arguments come readily to mind. What should be said about the case of a person who initially says 'yes' to a proposition on the basis of an argument which has sufficient plausibility to produce hesitant assent, and then discovers a demonstrative proof of that same proposition, one which establishes the necessity of the proposition, leaving no room either for deception of the assenter or for hesitation by him? Is this not a case in which, contrary to Lokert's dictum which I have just quoted, inevident assent becomes evident? And should we not say likewise as regards a case in which a person first accepts a proposition hesitantly on the basis of a probable argument and then has a visual experience of the kind which underpins evident assent to that same proposition? Surely we should say here also that the proposition has not changed but instead the mode of assent has; what was inevident has become evident. Perhaps Lokert's answer to these points would be that an assent of one kind has not *become* another; instead an assent of one kind has been *replaced* by an assent of another. But he does not supply an argument in support of this particular deployment of the distinction between becoming and replacement.

Where does faith stand in relation to evident assent and opinion? According to our late-medieval Scots it stands in an intermediate position, sharing a feature possessed by each of them and possessing in addition a feature which distinguishes it logically from both the others. Faith and evident assent have this in common, that each is given without hesitation. Faith and opinion have this in common, that they are inevident. But in what sense is faith inevident if an assent of faith is given unhesitantly? The question takes us to the heart of the matter.

It should be remembered that evident assent and opinion share the feature of being naturally caused. The alternative to natural causation is free causation. We are back to the great divide, between intellect and will, investigated by Scotus. Sometimes we say 'yes' on the basis of an exercise of intellect where the will is not engaged, for example, where we say 'yes' to a proposition because it is seen to follow logically from a set of propositions to which we have already assented. The point is that it was generally acknowledged that not every assent is like that. Many are based in part upon an act of will. Gilbert Crab of Aberdeen is helpful on this matter. He writes as follows: 'Some acts are natural, others are free. A natural act is one which is produced necessarily by a necessity of nature when everything requisite for its production is in place. For example, seeing is a natural act in relation to the faculty of sight . . . But a free act is one which is produced only contingently when everything necessary for its production is in place, for example an act of will.'[11] And this distinction, between natural acts and free ones, is then applied by Crab to the two ways of saying 'yes', evident assent and the assent of faith. In particular, he elucidates as follows: 'Faith is freely caused, because an act of will is required for it to be caused.'[12]

But even knowing that an assent of faith is a free act and not merely a natural one, we still need to determine what aspect of the assent is subject to will. Are all aspects of it? Well, not according to Lokert and his friends. They hold that saying 'yes' as an act of faith has two partial causes, one natural and the other free. It will be helpful here to focus on the fact that for those philosophers an opinion is never a purely irrational assent. Every opinion is based upon some premiss or other, though the premiss is not sufficient to justify an evident assent to the conclusion. An opinion is always based upon what was termed a *motivum probabile*, that is, grounds sufficiently strong to justify the person in saying 'yes' so long as his assent is merely hesitant (*tantum formidolosus*). Faith was said to have precisely the same sort of basis as opinion has, that is, a *motivum probabile*, and hence every assent of faith is supported by grounds sufficiently strong to justify only a hesitant assent. But there is then a second stage in which the person wills to adhere firmly to the proposition which is supported by the *motivum probabile* and wills also not to seek reasons for holding the opposite position.[13]

Since the person who has exercised his will in this way adheres firmly to the proposition in question, his assent is unhesitant. But it does not follow from this that by an act of will the assent which began as an opinion has become evident assent. The reason for this is that evident assent is caused by purely natural causes whereas faith is caused not only by natural causes but also by a free cause, namely an act of will. Causes of the two sorts *concurrunt* – they cooperate with each other in producing assent. It is on this basis that faith was seen as located between evident assent and opinion. As with evident assent faith is unhesitant, and as with opinion the natural cause which contributes to its production is a *motivum probabile*.

Two things in particular come under the heading of *motivum probabile*, namely authority and testimony. A person reports an event that he has witnessed, and I believe him. Though he might be speaking falsely about what he saw, even speaking falsely in saying that he was a witness at all, I have no reason to think he is speaking falsely, so I trust him. Part of what is involved in my trusting him is that my assent to the proposition that the events took place as reported is unhesitant. And my unhesitant assent is partially caused by an act of will. I decide to trust him. If I were not to decide to trust him, but instead were to allow nature to take its course by saying 'yes' with only the degree of hesitation warranted by the evidence, then my assent might indeed be hesitant. It would, in the technical sense of the term, be only an opinion of mine that the events occurred as reported.

For our late-medieval Scots any proposition to which we say 'yes' as a matter of faith is a proposition to which we have antecedent grounds for giving assent. I sometimes hear the phrase 'blind faith'. I am not certain what the phrase means though I am certain that it is a term of disparagement. But if it signifies an assent of faith given by a person who does not have antecedent reason for giving at least hesitant assent, then John Mair and his friends would without doubt dismiss the concept of blind faith as self-contradictory. In other words if the premises are insufficiently strong to support at least an opinion that the proposition is true, then there is no room for faith in its truth.

There are propositions to which we would, more or less hesitantly, say 'no' – propositions, in other words, from which we dissent though without assurance. We can by an act of will turn that hesitant 'no' round to a hesitant 'yes'. A further act of will can firm up that hesitant 'yes' to an unhesitant one. To reach purely by an act of will a hesitant, or even an unhesitant assent, from a hesitant dissent is perfectly possible and indeed all too human. But if we say 'yes' hesitantly as a result of an act of will, then that assent is not an opinion. And if on that basis we then say 'yes' unhesitantly as a result of an act of will, then we are not saying 'yes' as an act of faith.

The two points that I have just made are strictly terminological. That is, first, if by an act of will a dissent is turned into a hesitant assent then it is incorrect to apply the term 'opinion' to that hesitant assent. And secondly, if that willed hesitant assent is then willed into being unhesitant assent then that latter assent is not correctly termed an act of faith. These points, however, though terminological, are not merely so, and are not to be despised. It is always important to write in such a way as to be understood, and our philosophers were seeking to establish the meanings of crucial terms so that they could make their substantive theological and philosophical points with reasonable assurance that they would be correctly understood as they picked their way over theological battlegrounds on their way to a clear statement, and a clear understanding, of the truths that save.

It is plain that any theologian, especially of the Pre-Reformation period, would have several powerful reasons for being interested in clear definitions of terms relating to faith. And in that case there is no cause for wonder that the meaning of the term 'faith' itself was thought an appropriate object of investigation. My task in this lecture has been to show the way in which some Scottish philosopher-theologians of the Pre-Reformation period sought to place the concept of faith within a complex network which included also the concepts of evident assent, opinion, reason, natural causation and, especially, intellect and will. Those Scottish philosophers would have rejected the concept of blind faith as self-contradictory, for all of them accepted as a conceptual truth the fact that an assent of faith has an evidential basis. This point gives rise to the question: When is faith reasonable? It is to that question that I shall devote the next lecture, which will also be the last.

NOTES

1. 'Quarumcunque rerum distinctarum quarum neutra est deus nec aliqua est pars alterius deus quamcunque posset [con]servare in rerum natura alia destructa. Et per consequens in intellectu Sortis potest conservare assensum nulla habita apprehensiva et sic assentiret nihil intelligendo.' (Of any pair whatever of distinct things of which neither is God and neither is a part of the other, God could preserve either member of the pair in nature while destroying the other. And in consequence He can preserve an assent in the intellect of Socrates though Socrates has had no apprehensive notion. Hence Socrates would assent though he had understood nothing.) Lokert, *Scriptum in materia noticiarum* sig.e 8 recto, col. 1.

2. 'Notitia evidens alias evidentia simpliciter dicta sic definitur: est assensus verus sine formidine a principiis intellectum necessitantibus causatus quo non est possibile intellectum assentire et in sic assentiendo decipi.' Mair, *In Primum Sententiarum* fol. 6 verso, col. 1. Mair immediately adds, in clarification of the form of the definition: 'Assensus ponitur loco generis cum omnis evidentia sit assensus et non [e]contra. Reliquae vero particulae ponuntur loco differentiae.' ('Assent' is posited as the genus since every evident notion is an assent and not vice versa. The remaining clauses indicate the specific differences.)

3. 'Assensus evidens est assensus verus naturaliter causatus sine formidine sive in sic assentiendo intellectus potest decipi sive non.' Cranston, *Tractatus noticiarum* sig.c 2 verso, col. 1.

4. 'Dicitur . . . sine formidine ad excludendam suspitionem [et] coniecturam.' Mair, *In Primum Sententiarum* fol. 6 verso, col. 1.

5. 'Deus potest corrumpere parietem albedine servata et aliis accidentibus in eisdem locis in quibus nunc sunt. Quo facto assentiendo sicut prius ego essem deceptus. Hoc tamen non naturaliter contingit.' (God can destroy the wall while preserving the whiteness and the other accidents where they now are; and if this were done, then, in assenting as before, I would be deceived. But this does not happen in nature.) Lokert, *Scriptum in materia noticiarum* sig.f 1 recto, col. 1.

6. 'Evidentia summa est assensus certus naturaliter causatus per quem in assentiendo impossibile est intellectum decipi nec naturali nec supernaturali potentia.' Crab, *Tractatus noticiarum* sig.c 6 recto, col. 1.

7. 'De nulla propositione necessaria habetur aliqua evidentia nisi absoluta. Postquam propositio est necessaria non est possibile per aliquam potentiam decipi assentiendo tali propositioni.' Lokert, *Scriptum in materia noticiarum* sig.e 8 verso, col. 2.

8. 'Assensus inevidens est assensus certus sine formidine mere libere causatus ut assensus huius: deus est trinus et unus. Non potest causari in intellectu humano sine imperio voluntatis. Et omnis talis assensus vocatur fides.

Dicit Augustinus ad propositum: nemo potest credere non volens.'
Cranston, *Tractatus noticiarum* sig.c 2 verso, col. 2.

9. 'Fides dupliciter capitur uno modo pro assensu propositionis praeceptae
in lege dei formaliter vel aequivalenter . . . Alio modo capitur pro omni
assensu libere causato propter auctoritatem dicentis sive sit praeceptum
sive non.' *Ibid*.

10. 'Et ex consequente nullus assensus evidens potest fieri inevidens nec
econtra.' Lokert, *Scriptum in materia noticiarum* sig.f 2 verso, col. 2.

11. 'Actuum alius est naturalis alius liber. Actus naturalis est actus qui positis
omnibus requisitis ad eius productionem necessario necessitate naturae
producitur ut visio est actus naturalis respectu potentiae visivae . . . Sed
actus liber est operatio quae positis omnibus requisitis ad eius productionem
mere contingenter producitur ut operatio voluntatis.' Crab, *Tractatus
terminorum moralium* sig.b 3 recto–verso.

12. 'Et sic fides libere causatur quia ad ipsum causandum requiritur actus
voluntatis.' Crab, *Tractatus noticiarum* sig.c 6 recto, col. 1.

13. 'Communior opinio inter doctores dicit assensum fidei causari a motivo
probabili hoc est ab assensu consequentiae et antecedentis aut praemissarum
opinativis vel quorum unus est opinativus et actu voluntatis quo aliquis
vult ita esse vel firmiter adhaerere tali propositioni et non quaerere rationes
ad oppositum, etc.' – An assent of faith is caused (1) by a probable motive
(*motivum probabile*), that is, by an assent both to an inference and to the
antecedent or premisses, where at least one of the assents is opinative,
and (2) by an act of will by which someone wills that things be thus [*sc.* as
stated in the conclusion of the inference] or wills to adhere firmly to that
proposition, and wills not to seek reasons for [accepting] the opposite,
etc. Lokert, *Scriptum in materia noticiarum* sig.f 5 recto, cols. 1–2.

Lecture 6

When is faith reasonable?

WE HAVE been investigating a definition of faith formulated and expounded by members of the circle of John Mair. I shall now take that investigation a stage further, and shall set the scene with a prefatory comment concerning the cultural context of the definition.

There were powerful reasons why those theologians were careful in their formulations. We should not lose sight of the fact that during the thirty years from 1503, amongst many other persons no less than fifteen members of the Faculty of Theology at the University of Paris were investigated by the Faculty for heresy. It was a period during which both John Mair and George Lokert were active members. Those whom Faculty commissions found guilty of heresy were handed over to the civil authorities for punishment, which could be deadly since it was a period when heresy in France was regarded as akin to treason against his very Christian majesty François 1er. Indeed George Lokert was one of those who sat on a Faculty commission convened to investigate one of Erasmus's works *A refutation of the erroneous censures of Noel Beda*. Erasmus was sufficiently wary to remain away from Paris during this period. His translator Louis de Berquin, confident of the protection of his patrons, was less wary. He was found guilty of heresy by the Faculty of Theology, and was handed over to the civil authorities who burned him at the stake before the Cathedral of Notre Dame. That happened in 1529. One year earlier, Patrick Hamilton, who had studied under members of John Mair's circle in Paris and St Andrews, was burned outside the College of St Salvator's in St Andrews, the college of which Mair was shortly thereafter to become provost.[1]

It has to be said therefore that not only the sovereign importance of the saving of souls, but also – and relatedly – the consequence of being judged to have published theological errors, were bound to make theologians very careful when investigating articles of faith. This care naturally governed their approach not only to the propositions to which the faithful assented in faith, but also to the concept of faith itself. One result was the definition which I expounded in the course of Lecture Five. The further examination of the definition that I shall now make will take the form of a clarification of the relation between on the one hand reason, and on the other hand faith, as the term is understood by Mair and his colleagues.

As with earlier lectures in this series, my starting point will be the teachings of Duns Scotus, presiding genius of Scottish philosophy. I have focused on Scotus's doctrines concerning will and intellect, observing that on his analysis the two faculties are really identical and differ only in form. That doctrine can be seen as a development of his insight regarding the special unity of the human mind. A person looks out upon the world both as a spectator and as an agent, seeking sometimes to understand the world and sometimes to change it. His mind has the form of a spectator in so far as he engages in acts of understanding, and it has the form of an agent in so far as he engages in acts of will. But it is one and the same mind that has these different forms. Scotus, as we saw, called these forms 'formalities', and argued that the metaphysical status of will and intellect is that of distinct formalities of one and the same reality, the mind which understands and wills.

In several places John Mair invokes William Ockham's demand that entities not be multiplied beyond necessity. The demand leaves its mark at crucial places in Mair's system, and I think that we are here dealing with one of those places, his refusal to see value in the concept of a formality of the mind. Whatever Scotus wanted to say about the formalities of will and intellect could in Mair's view be better said by speaking in terms of acts or operations of the mind. To say that a faculty of will exists is to say that a mind can will, and to say that a faculty of intellect exists is to say that a mind can understand. If it is the one mind that acts in these two ways, then the faculties of will and intellect of that mind are identical with each other because they are identical with that mind.

John Mair thus subscribes as fully as does Scotus himself to the doctrine of the irrefragable metaphysical unity of the human mind. He may indeed have thought that he subscribed more fully to it, on the grounds that the unity of the mind must be less than perfect if the mind has distinct formalities.

I remain sceptical however over whether this is a substantive disagreement between Scotus and Mair, or merely a terminological one. An agent able to perform acts of different kinds takes different forms when it performs those acts. The forms are not realities separate or separable from the acts they inform. I think that if Scotus had not called the forms of intellect and will 'formalities', but had instead, and without changing his philosophical stance, spoken of the different ways in which the mind changes in the course of the performance of these different sorts of act, then Mair would not have objected to Scotus's account. Mair on the contrary understood Scotus's 'formalities' to be features or elements of the mind over and above the changes that take place in it when it wills an act or understands a proposition. I think that in so interpreting Scotus Mair was in error, and that there is in consequence hardly any daylight, if any at all, between the theories of the two men.

Central to their theories is the idea that the human mind is an irrefragible unity. This unity is manifest in countless ways, and no more so than in the kind of act we have been calling *assensus fidei* – saying 'yes' as an act of faith. In speaking of unity in respect of this sort of assent I have in mind the idea discussed in the preceding lecture, that faith is the product of two causes, an act of intellect and an act of will. This is not a matter of two causes, acts of will and intellect, which are temporally antecedent to the assent of faith which is their joint effect. On the contrary the willing and the understanding enter into the assent of faith as parts of its nature, intellect providing the content of the act and will providing its form, the free assenting. These two parts are separable by an act of philosophical analysis, though they are not separable in nature. In particular the act of freely assenting cannot occur except as having a content, that to which we assent, and that content is provided by the intellect.

The doctrine that the assent of faith is the product of those two causes is central to late-medieval investigations of the nature of faith. Let us therefore look more closely into the relation between faith on the one hand and intellect and will on the other. It will quickly be seen that this gives us a helpful perspective on the question of when faith is reasonable.

That John Mair attaches special importance to the idea that an act of will is a partial cause of faith is attested by the fact that the idea is presented in folio 1 of Book One of his *Commentary on the Sentences of Peter Lombard*. Without doubt that *Commentary* is the greatest of Mair's theological writings. He begins by discussing the way in which faith is acquired by the *viator*, the wayfarer on his earthly pilgrimage, and he therefore has to deal with the question of what the pilgrim has acquired in acquiring faith. Peter Lombard, whose *Sententiae* was the most influential theological work of the Middle Ages, defines 'faith' as 'the power by means of which things which are not seen are believed'. To which Mair adds this comment: '"Faith" is not taken to refer to all things which are not seen, but, as St Augustine says, it is taken to refer only to those things belief in which pertains to religion.'[2]

But if those things pertaining to religion are not seen, why are they believed? It cannot be that the evidence for them determines the intellect to believe, since in saying that they are not seen the point being made is precisely that there is insufficient evidence to compel the intellect's assent. Mair argues that the only possible explanation for the occurrence of belief is that the will plays a role, and that it is the invisibility of the things pertaining to religion that, so to say, creates a space within which the will has room to act.

John Mair finds a proof text for this doctrine in Romans 10.16, at a point where Paul the apostle is himself using Isaiah 53.1 as a proof text. Mair, relying on a Bible other than the Vulgate, though I do not know which, quotes the verse: 'O Lord, who believes what we have heard?', and he refers us to the *Glossa Ordinaria*, which asks why the Jews do not believe, and which replies that it is because they will not to. And hence, concludes Mair, to will not to believe is incompatible with the production of faith, and hence will cooperates in the production of faith.[3]

'And again', continues Mair, 'since God obliges us to believe, and does not oblige us to do what transcends our powers, believing and not believing will both be free acts.' In support of this position he quotes St Augustine: 'Someone can enter a church while willing not to. He can approach the altar while willing not to. He can receive the sacrament while willing not to. But he cannot believe unless he wills to.'[4] Finally in this compilation of evidence concerning the tightness of the link between faith and will, Mair quotes Mark 16.16: 'Qui vero non crediderit condemnabitur' – 'He who does not believe will be condemned.' (I refer to the Vulgate's verse numbering here, since neither the Revised Standard Version nor the New English Bible includes this verse). To the verse: 'He who does not believe will be condemned', Mair adds the comment: 'There is no precept unless the will cooperates in its implementation.'[5] That is, God would not condemn us for not performing an act the performance of which is not under our voluntary control. Yet God would condemn us for not obeying His commands. From which Mair concludes that obeying God's commands, all of them, are acts subject to our will. Since, as we have now been reminded, there is a divine precept that we believe, that is, that we have faith, it follows that whether or not we have faith is subject to our will. It would appear to follow that faith is located in the will.

For John Mair the situation is rather more complicated. He wonders in which faculty, will or intellect, faith should be located, and his response makes it clear that he believes it to be in both for it is a product of two partial causes. Since one of the two partial causes of an assent of faith is an act of opinative assent, and the other partial cause is the act by which the hesitation of opinion is made firm or unhesitant, it should be concluded that the assent of faith is located in both faculties, intellect and will. It is in intellect because the inference of an opinative conclusion from the premises of the probable argument is a purely intellectual act. Will contributes nothing to this part of the assent of faith since the premises of such an inference are a purely natural cause, and therefore not at all a free cause, of the conclusion. In addition will is a partial cause of the assent of faith, because the act of rendering firm or unhesitant the hesitant assent of opinion is a free act and not one that is merely naturally caused.

Nevertheless, we should recognise the relative ordering of these two partial causes. The definition of faith that we have been considering has the form of a definition *per genus et differentiam* – it states the genus of the species we call 'assent of faith' and then indicates the features that differentiate that species from other species in that genus. An assent of faith is generically an assent, and assent is essentially an intellectual act. What differentiates the assent of faith is the role of the will in giving firmness to what otherwise would be an opinative and therefore a merely hesitant assent. Primary location depends upon the generic feature of the species and secondary location depends upon features which differentiate the species from other species in the same genus. It follows that the assent of faith is located primarily in the intellect and secondarily in the will. Thus we find Mair affirming: 'Since believing [*credere*] inheres in the intellect and is an assent, it is really an act of intellect and primarily inheres in that faculty. And if *per possibile* or *per impossibile* intellect were separated from will, the assent of faith would inhere in intellect and not in will.'[6] Mair's point is however that even though separation of the two faculties would leave the assent of faith in intellect rather than in will, nevertheless what would be in intellect would not be precisely an assent of faith but just an assent of opinion. For without the act of will the assent could not be of faith. Mair is therefore committed to the doctrine that though the assent is primarily in the intellect, for without an act of intellect there would be no assent, it is secondarily in the will for, granted the occurrence of the act of intellect, there is then required an act of will to transform the assent into one of faith.

Let us focus upon the doctrine that faith is located primarily in the intellect. A link between faith and intellect is of course invoked in Anselm's projected title to his *Proslogion* – *Fides quaerens intellectum* ('Faith seeking understanding'). For the last time in this series of lectures I shall turn to St Anselm's phrase. He let his intellect play upon the object of his faith and sought, in a work unsurpassed in philosophy, to clarify the nature of the divine existence. His faith sought understanding, and by the end of the intellectual activity that found expression in the *Proslogion* his concept of the divine existence was more deeply informed by reason. In that sense, which is not a negligible one, his faith had become more reasonable.

From this perspective a person's faith is reasonable to the extent that it is a faith thought through, so that the credal propositions to which assent is given are well understood by the assenter. He is not merely saying 'yes', but also has a clear grasp of what it is to which he is saying 'yes'. On this account a person's faith is unreasonable if he has little or no understanding of these religious formulae to which he gives his assent. He has not sufficiently mixed his intellect with the formulae.

This account of reasonable faith gives rise to a second distinction. It is one thing to have a deep understanding of a proposition to which we say 'yes' as an act of faith and it is another to recognise that we have grounds for giving that assent. Having faith is not merely a matter of understanding a proposition but also of assenting to it. And granted that the proposition is well understood we can also ask whether it is reasonable to say 'yes' to it.

We have already observed that from the perspective of the late-medieval Scots upon whom these lectures have been focused an assent of faith can conceptually speaking occur only in the context of an inference or argument. To say 'yes' as an act of faith requires having reason for saying 'yes' hesitantly to the proposition. It is not merely that there is a reason why the person should say yes; he has made that reason his own. It is *his* reason for assenting. The assenter has, then, antecedently a *motivum probabile*, a reason he recognises as a plausible one, for holding the proposition as a matter of opinion. It does not require faith for him to give hesitant assent. Whatever we should call the act of will by which a person moves, without additional evidence, from a 'no' or from nothing to a hesitant 'yes', it should not be called faith. Faith is reached by moving from the hesitant assent of opinion to unhesitant assent. If for a person's assent of faith to be reasonable it is sufficient that he have evidence sufficient by itself to support a hesitant assent, then by definition, that is, by the late-medieval definition I have been expounding, all faith is reasonable.

And yet there is something bizarre about this claim. Let us accept, with John Mair and his colleagues, that an assent of faith has some rational basis, sufficient at least to support an opinion. Let us also remind ourselves that they held that an assent of faith is a product of two partial causes, one natural and the other free. The natural cause produces an opinion. As a result of the free cause, the act of will, not only do we say 'yes'; we also cease to look for reasons for saying 'no', for the matter has been settled. 'Yes' has won.

It is the gap between the hesitation of opinion and the firmness of faith that here interests me. What justifies the move from the one to the other? The answer seems to be that nothing does. The evidence, such as it is, takes us to the stage of assenting hesitantly. It is will and not intellect that takes us further. If the evidence were sufficiently strong by itself to compel us to give unhesitant assent we should no longer be talking about faith but about some other cognitive state. Evidence, after all, counts as a natural cause, not a free one. And without a free cause an assent of faith cannot be given. And in so far as we cannot provide grounds, in the form of evidence, justifying the move from hesitant assent to unhesitant, the move is not sanctioned by reason, and to that extent it is unreasonable. That is why I said there is something bizarre about the claim that every assent of faith is reasonable. The premisses that I have just produced appear to support the conclusion that no assent of faith is reasonable.

We should not lose sight of the fact that the conclusion of this argument is not that it is unreasonable to give an assent when we give an assent of faith; the conclusion is instead that the lack of hesitation in giving that assent is unreasonable. For it is not the act of assenting, but the fact that the assent is given unhesitantly, that is not sanctioned by reason. Is the absence of justification for the lack of hesitation sufficient to make the assent of faith unreasonable? If it is, then this is presumably on the basis of the principle that an act as a whole is unreasonable if any part of it is not sanctioned by reason. I am not enthusiastic about this principle. I agree that it would be unreasonable to assent to a proposition in the absence of sufficient evidence to justify even a hesitant assent, but there is clearly a difference in kind between assenting firmly in the absence of evidence justifying any sort of assent, and assenting firmly in the presence of evidence justifying an assent of sorts even if only a hesitant one. I do not think that an assent has to be fully supported by evidence every inch of the way in order to be sufficiently supported to count as reasonable. To say otherwise would be to insist upon an unreasonable criterion of reasonableness.

It was noted in Lecture Five that authority and testimony fall under the heading of *motivum probabile*, that is, the kind of evidence that motivates us to give opinative assent. Authority and testimony are not quite the same thing, but they are very closely related. A person who testifies to something speaks as a witness. Suppose that such a person tells me that a given event occurred. On the basis of his testimony I form the opinion that it did indeed occur, that is, I give my hesitant assent. But, as we have seen, it was the view of Lokert and his friends that I can decide to trust the person, take him fully at his word, throw in my lot with his testimony, and give not hesitant but wholehearted assent to what I have been told. An authority on a topic is treated as a witness to the truth; to recognise someone as an authority is to treat what he says as testimony to the truth. Even without investigating his arguments we give assent, at least hesitant assent, to his conclusions. And how can we not, if we accept him as speaking with authority? The link between testimony and authority is thus plain.

Authority, considered in this light, was central to the whole enterprise of philosophy and theology in the Middle Ages. One can hardly read any dozen lines by any medieval philosopher or theologian without meeting with an *auctoritas* – an authoritative text. We are, again and again, told that support for a given proposition is provided by Aristotle or St Paul or St Augustine, or an Old Testament prophet, who said much the same thing as is expressed in the proposition, or who said something from which the proposition in question can be deduced.

That an authority said something is never treated as conclusive evidence of the truth of some other proposition, but it is evidence of sorts, a reason for assenting to it even if not a conclusive reason.[7] It becomes, so to say, the default position, something to accept unless and until a contrary proposition can be shown to have a firmer basis. Aquinas discusses this matter in the *Summa Theologiae* pt. 1, q. 1, a.8, in the course of his enquiry into whether the science of sacred doctrine proceeds by way of argument. It is easy to construct a case for saying that it should not proceed by way of argument. For, he reminds us, St Ambrose declares: 'Remove arguments from the place where faith is sought' (*De fide Catholica* 51.1). But it is especially in sacred doctrine that faith is sought. Hence sacred doctrine is not argumentative. In any case, Aquinas continues, if it is argumentative, then at any rate it surely does not proceed on the basis of arguments from authority. They are ill suited to the dignity of sacred doctrine for, as Boethius declares, arguments (*loci*) from authority are the shakiest (*infirmissimi*) of all.

There is, of course, an air of paradox surrounding the fact that Aquinas argues on the basis of the authority of Boethius for the claim that authority is the weakest of all arguments. But an air of paradox is not the same thing as a contradiction, and Aquinas is not here guilty of contradiction. He begins by stating that arguments from authority are especially appropriate to sacred doctrine because the principles of the doctrine are acquired by revelation and hence the doctrine itself should be believed on the authority of those to whom the revelation was granted. It is true that arguments from human authority are the weakest, but an argument founded upon the authority of divine revelation is the strongest (*efficacissimus*).[8]

The matter is not entirely plain sailing however. For, of course, God's word is in need of interpretation and it is the interpretation of human beings upon which we must rely. It follows that the argument from authority is always to be treated as sufficient to ground only an opinion, never to ground an evident assent. That Aristotle asserted a given proposition is a reason for saying 'yes' to it, but only hesitantly, for the argument from authority can always be trumped by an argument which appeals, say, to a logical principle. In short, since Aristotle or St Augustine, whose writings have informed the thinking of civilised people for centuries, have asserted a given proposition, it is reasonable to accept the proposition on their authority, so long, of course, as one always recognises that at a later stage a reason may emerge for rejecting their word.

In practice authorities were rarely shown to have been wrong, for if on a not wildly implausible interpretation of what they said they can be shown to have been correct, then why not adopt that interpretation?

To do so would not require one to be excessively charitable, for after all it was from such thinkers that their successors gained, in large measure, the intellectual standards which they in their turn used in order to establish the truth. This outlook does not make it impossible to reject an *auctoritas,* but it certainly requires one to produce strong evidence on behalf of a contrary position before saying even hesitantly that the *auctoritas* is wrong.

Even if it is reasonable to assent, though hesitantly, to a proposition if it is supported by an authority, what should be said about the further stage, the exercise of will in the direction of saying 'yes' not hesitantly but firmly? Surely that is unreasonable? Yet it may not be entirely so. Lokert speaks about the assent of faith as an assent made by a person who wills to adhere firmly to a given proposition and wills also not to seek reasons for supporting the opposite position.[9] Since the person has assented firmly, there is no reason why he should seek evidence in support of the opposite position. But it is an important feature of Lokert's doctrine that he does not describe the person of faith as refusing to countenance evidence to the contrary if he happens upon it. If he meets with such evidence then, as a reasonable person, he will treat it on its merits and may withdraw his assent of faith. In this respect his behaviour contrasts with that of a person who gives evident assent to a proposition. Such a person may reasonably consider himself entitled to disregard subsequent evidence to the contrary. Since he is already in possession of overwhelming evidence in favour of the proposition to which he gives evident assent, it follows that evidence to the contrary must be in some way faulty, or at any rate of insufficient weight to overturn his assent. Plainly a person who says 'yes' as an act of faith is quite differently situated in relation to evidence which works against his assent. He would indeed be acting unreasonably if he rejected out of hand evidence which conflicted with his faith.

I have now spoken of three ways in which an assent of faith might be said to be reasonable. The first way requires a person to have mixed his intellectual labour with the proposition at issue, and to have acquired a deep understanding of it. St Anselm's investigation into the nature of divine existence is a paradigm of such intellectual labour. The second way requires an assent of faith to be based on an inference whose premises are sufficient to support at least hesitant assent to the proposition in which faith is subsequently placed. And the third way requires the person who says 'yes' as an act of faith not to seek to make himself impervious to appeals to his reason, where the appeals take the form of the display of evidence against his faith.

Willingness to countenance evidence to the contrary is reasonable in virtue of what some philosophers termed the 'obscurity' associated with faith. Mair's colleague at Paris, Gervaise Waim, affirmed that: 'faith is imperfect because it is not clear assent as evident assent is'.[10] He explains: 'Clarity in truth or falsity is a reason why we assent to or dissent from some propositions as soon as we know their terms. But there are propositions whose truth is so obscure that the intellect would be unable to assent to them unless it had help from somewhere else.'[11]

Waim's position therefore is that assent to an evident proposition is more perfect than an assent of faith. An evident proposition is recognised as true as soon as the proposition is understood. The will plays no role. In the case of our saying 'yes' as an act of faith, our understanding of the proposition is insufficient by itself to enable us to assent without hesitation. Its truth therefore is obscure to us. In virtue of this obscurity the firm assent, when made, is imperfect, because obscurity is an imperfection.

Some may wish to take a different approach and to draw a different conclusion. It might be pointed out that it takes more to give firm assent to a proposition whose truth is obscure to us than to one whose truth is clear. Since the intellect is involved in such an assent and since the will also is involved, more of the human spirit is expressed in an assent of faith than in evident assent, and in one respect therefore an assent of faith is more perfect than is an evident assent.

This conclusion, however, must be held lightly. Assent to an evident proposition may represent a great triumph of the spirit for, as Aquinas reminds us, what is evident in itself is not always evident to us,[12] and a considerable effort of will might be required before a person is in a position to give evident assent. And on the other hand the acceptance of a proposition on faith may be a product of laziness – indicating a preference for asking an authority rather than for taking the available step of thinking the matter out for oneself and thereby becoming an eye witness to the truth, rather than trusting someone else who *is* an eye witness to it.

I should like to make one final point about the relation between faith and reason, a point which applies as much to non-religious as to religious faith, though it is really the latter that I have in mind here. There are cases in which it is reasonable to say 'yes' as an act of faith. Let us suppose that we recognise a person as speaking with authority when he says that there is a God. That person may himself be assenting as an act of faith to the message he transmits, for he himself places his faith in some other person's word. A chain can be formed in which all links after the first say 'yes' as an act of faith on the basis of their recognition of the authoritative nature of the word of a preceding link. But those later links in the chain cannot suppose that the first in the chain faithfully accepted God's word for it that God exists. He would need to know that it was God he encountered. And how would he know that?

At the start of Genesis 12 we read: 'Now the Lord had said unto Abram, Get thee out of thy country, and from thy kindred, and from thy father's house, unto a land that I will show thee. . . . So Abram departed as the Lord had spoken unto him.' This was one of the great moments in human history, yet we are told so little. There is nothing that I would more like to know about anything than the content of the experience that Abraham underwent. He could no more have been taking God's word for it that God exists than you my audience, now, can take my word for it that I do. It is too late for you to take my word for it that I do, because you have met me. It is I whom you already know to exist who would be telling you that I do. Likewise God's saying 'I exist' could not have conveyed to Abraham information that he did not already have as a result of encountering God. There was thus no room for such an act by Abraham as taking God's word for it that He exists. Abraham was no doubt a man of faith in respect of his acceptance of God's word that his seed would be a mighty nation, but he was not a man of faith in respect of knowing that God was addressing him. On the contrary Abraham participated in the event that others would believe occurred because they had faith in Abraham's testimony.

It is no accident that in discussing faith the late-medieval philosophers link authority and testimony so closely. What I have just been speaking about is the situation of any person who accepts something on authority. He cannot suppose that what he accepts on that basis has only ever been accepted on that same basis. Someone must have a different sort of evidence for the truth of the proposition that others accept on authority. If I take someone's word for it that a given mathematical proposition is true, I must suppose that someone can prove that it is, or at least that he has a rational insight into its truth, unlike myself who can assert with confidence that it is true, not because I can see that it is but because someone who can has reported his findings.

I think that this is a logical point, just as it is a logical point that if I accept something on the authority of a witness it is because I believe that the witness saw what he reports as having happened and was not simply relying on the authority of another for the account that he gives me. At this logical level there is no difference between religious and non-religious faith. The difference emerges when we seek clarification concerning the nature of the experience that the witness had. If someone reports the words of a human being he encountered, we can imagine the meeting. But how are we to imagine or conceive Abraham's encounter with God? I shall not attempt here to answer that question. But Lord Gifford would be well pleased if a future Gifford lecturer took that further step.

In these lectures I have been exploring a set of ideas that were to the fore in philosophical and theological discussions in Scotland at the time of the founding of the University of Aberdeen. Much of what I have been saying would indeed have been said to those earliest generations of Aberdeen students, and it was certainly familiar to Hector Boece, first principal of the University of Aberdeen and friend and colleague of John Mair at the University of Paris. Especially familiar to Boece and his students were those medieval Scottish discussions of the concept of faith that I have been exploring. I argued at the outset that for medieval philosophers faith was the space of philosophy. For not only was much of their philosophising conducted in the pages of their theological treatises, but more importantly their faith gave direction to their philosophy, and gave urgency to it. They did not philosophise as a form of entertainment. Their philosophy related directly to pastoral concerns regarding the salvation of souls.

But as well as the content of their faith, they also attended to its form, the fact that it was faith, and not demonstrative knowledge or mere opinion. What, then, is it to give an assent of faith rather than of demonstrative knowledge or opinion? The answer provided by the Pre-Reformation Scots was given in terms of a particular relation between acts of intellect and will. Such acts, and the relations between them, were examined in great detail by Duns Scotus, and of especial interest are his conclusions regarding will as the faculty of freedom, where freedom is understood as the power to produce opposite effects.

Yet do we have such a power? Many of the medieval discussions regarding the possibility of freedom occur in the theological context of an account of God as omniscient. If God knows from all eternity what we shall do, does His knowledge leave us with any room to manoeuvre? Surely God's omniscience implies determinism. John Ireland, whose arguments on behalf of the faith are influenced by Scotus, sought to rebut this line of attack, for he recognised that the faith would be a sham if the doctrine of divine omniscience were indeed incompatible with human freedom. Distinguishing between divine intellect and divine will, he argues that God wills into existence creatures with will, and then leaves us to do what we will to do. He knows our acts but does not will that we perform them. He commands us, but does not will us to obey. If He willed us to obey then we would do so for what God wills to be will be, but we are free to disobey.

John Ireland rebutted the claim that our faculty of free will is a sham. Such a rebuttal provided space for the analysis of the concept of faith that was made by John Mair and his colleagues. The assent of faith, on their analysis, constitutes a special sort of unity of acts of intellect and will, two faculties which, as Scotus teaches, form a special sort of unity in the human soul.

In those late-medieval writings, Scotus's shadow is clearly discernible, even when he is being directly contradicted, as sometimes he is, by members of Mair's circle. Scotus is the presiding genius of Scottish philosophy, and he was assuredly in ghostly attendance upon those faithful men in the companionable circle of John Mair as they argued their way through the decades that preceded the Scottish Reformation and the establishment of a new order in this country.

NOTES

1. Events referred to in this paragraph are discussed in A. Broadie, *George Lokert: Late Scholastic Logician* ch. 1.
2. 'Tertio modo accipitur [sc. credere] proprie pro assentire sine formidine propositionibus quae pertinent ad salutem. De quo dicit Magister libro iii, dist.xxiii, cap.ii: Fides est virtus qua creduntur quae non videntur. Quod tamen non de omnibus quae non videntur accipiendum est sed de his tantum quae credere ut ait Augustinus in *Enchiridio* ad religionem pertinet.' Mair, *In Primum Sententiarum* fol. 1 recto, col. 2.
3. 'Pia affectio enim supponit pro actu voluntatis connotando quod velit illud quod concernit religionem et nolit illud quod ei adversatur ut patet *ad Romanos* x ubi apostolus introducit illud *Esaie* liii: Domine quis credit auditui nostro, ubi Glossa Ordinaria proponens dubitationem quare

Judaei non credunt dicit quod non credunt quia nolunt. Et sic nolle repugnat generationi fidei et per consequens velle ad generationem eiusdem concurrit.' Mair, *In Primum Sententiarum* fol. 1 verso, cols. 1–2.

4. 'Rursus cum deus obliget nos ad credendum et non obliget nos ad illud quod transcendit vires nostras liberum erit credere et non credere secundum illud Beati Augustini *Homilia* xxvi: Intrare ecclesiam potest quis nolens, accedere ad altare nolens, recipere potest sacramentum nolens, credere autem non nisi volens.' Mair, *In Primum Sententiarum* fol. 1 verso, col. 2.

5. 'Nullum enim est praeceptum nisi ad eius impletionem concurrat voluntas.' *Ibid.*

6. 'Sed quia [credere] inhaeret intellectui et est assensus realiter est actus intellectus et ei primo inhaeret. Et si per possibile vel impossibile intellectus separaretur a voluntate intellectui ille assensus inhaereret et non voluntati.' *Ibid.*

7. For discussion of this point see C. F. J. Martin 'The argument from authority', in Peter Geach, *et al. The Past and the Present: Problems of Understanding: A Philosophical and Historical Enquiry.*

8. 'Dicendum quod argumentari ex auctoritate est maxime proprium huius doctrinae [*sc.* sacrae doctrinae] eo quod principia huius doctrinae per revelationem habentur. Et sic oportet quod credatur auctoritati eorum quibus revelatio facta est. Nec hoc derogat dignitati huius doctrinae nam licet locus ab auctoritate quae fundatur super ratione humana sit infirmissimus locus tamen ab auctoritate quae fundatur super revelatione divina est efficacissimus.' Aquinas, *Summa Theologiae* 1, 1, 8 ad 2.

9. 'Communior opinio inter doctores dicit assensum fidei causari a . . . actu voluntatis quo aliquis vult ita esse vel firmiter adhaerere tali propositioni et non quaerere rationes ad oppositum, etc.' Lokert, *Scriptum in materia noticiarum* sig.f 5 recto, col. 2.

10. 'Fides habet imperfectionem ex eo quia non est assensus clarus sicut evidentia.' Waim, *Tractatus noticiarum* sig.i 1 verso, col. 1.

11. 'Claritas in veritate vel falsitate est causa quare alicui propositioni statim cognitis terminis assentimus vel dissentimus. Aliqua vero est cuius veritas est tam obscura sic quod ratione talis obscuritatis in veritate intellectus non habito subsidio aliunde non poterit illi assentire.' Waim, *Tractatus noticiarum* sig.h 3 recto, col. 1.

12. 'Dicendum quod contingit aliquid esse per se notum dupliciter uno modo secundum se et non quoad nos alio modo secundum se et quoad nos' – Something can be self-evident in one or other of two ways, either self-evident in itself and not to us, or self-evident both in itself and to us. Aquinas, *Summa Theologiae* 1, 2, 1 c.

Bibliography

PRIMARY SOURCES

Abbreviations

AUL   Aberdeen University Library
BL   British Library
BN   Bibliothèque Nationale
Bodl   Bodleian Library, Oxford
CL   Columbina Library, Seville
CUL   Cambridge University Library
EUL   Edinburgh University Library
GUL   Glasgow University Library
ML   Mitchell Library, Glasgow
NLS   National Library of Scotland
StA   St Andrews University Library
StJ   St John's College Library, Cambridge
TCL   Trinity College Library, Dublin

Adam of Dryburgh, in J.-P. Migne *Patrologia Latina,* Paris 1844–64 (221 vols.), vol. 153, cols. 799–884; vol. 184, cols. 869–80; vol. 198, cols. 91–872.

Anselm of Canterbury, *S. Anselmi Cantuariensis Archiepiscopi Opera Omnia,* ed. F. S. Schmitt, O.S.B., Edinburgh 1946. Volume 1 contains *Monologion* and *Proslogion.*

Aquinas, Thomas, *De electione humana* = *Quaestio* 6 in *Quaestiones disputatae de malo,* in *Quaestiones Disputatae* vol. 2, 9th rev. edn., Turin/Rome 1953.

Aquinas, Thomas, *Summa Theologiae,* Turin/Rome 1948.

Boece, Hector, *Explicatio quorundam vocabulorum ad cognitionem dialectices conducentium opera Hectoris Boethii philosophi insignis in lucem edita,* Paris c. 1519 (sole extant copy in GUL).

Boece, Hector, *Murthlacensium et Aberdonensium episcoporum vitae*, ed. and tr. J. Moir (New Spalding Club publications, 12), Aberdeen 1894.

Crab, Gilbert, *Tractatus noticiarum*, Paris c. 1503 (in NLS).

Crab, Gilbert, *Tractatus terminorum moralium*, Paris c. 1512 (in StA); c. 1514 (in Bodl).

Crab, Gilbert, *Tractatus lucidus terminorum*, Paris 1524 (in CUL).

Cranston, David, *Tractatus noticiarum parvulis et provectis utilissimus*, Paris 1517 (in AUL).

Duns Scotus, John, *Opera Omnia* ed. L. Wadding, Paris 1891–5.

Duns Scotus, John, *Opera Omnia* ed. C. Balić, Civitas Vaticana 1950–.

Duns Scotus, John, *God and Creatures: The Quodlibetal Questions,* trs. F. Alluntis and A. B. Wolter, Princeton 1975.

Duns Scotus, John, *Duns Scotus on the Will and Morality*, Selected and translated with an Introduction by Allan B. Wolter, O.F.M., Washington D.C. 1986.

Galbraith, Robert, *Quadrupertitum in oppositiones conversiones hypotheticas et modales Magistri Roberti Caubraith*, Paris 1510 (in AUL, BL, Bodl); Paris 1516 (in BN, GUL).

Gregory of Rimini, *Super Primum et Secundum Sententiarum*, Venice 1522. Reprinted St Bonaventure, N.Y. 1955.

Henry of Ghent, *Opera Omnia*, eds R. Macken, *et al.*, Leiden 1979–.

Ireland, John, *The Meroure of Wyssdome by Johannes de Irlandia*, vol. I, ed. C. MacPherson, Edinburgh 1926; vol. II, ed. J. F. Quinn, Edinburgh 1965; vol. III, ed. C. McDonald, Edinburgh 1900.

John Duns Scotus *see under* Duns Scotus, John.

Ledelh, Jacobus (James Liddell), *Tractatus conceptuum et signorum*, Paris 1495 (sole extant copy in NLS).

Lokert, George, *Scriptum in materia noticiarum*, Paris 1514 (in EUL, NLS); Paris 1520 (in CUL); Paris 1524 (in Bodl).

Lokert, George, *Questio subtillissima de futuro contingenti*, Paris c. 1524 (in CLS).

Mair, John, *In primum Sententiarum*, Paris 1519 (in Bodl, GUL, NLS, StJ, TCL).

Mair, John, *In secundum Sententiarum*, Paris 1519 (in Bodl, CUL, GUL).

Mair, John, *Editio Joannis Maioris . . . Super tertium Sententiarum*, Paris 1517 (in CUL, GUL, NLS, StA, TCL).

Mair, John, *In quartum Sententiarum*, Paris 1509 (in BL, CUL, GUL, StA); Paris 1512 (in AUL); Paris 1519 (in AUL, Bodl, CUL, GUL, NLS, StA).

Bibliography

Mair, John, *Historia Maioris Britanniae tam Angliae quam Scotiae*, Paris 1521. Translated as *A History of Greater Britain as well England as Scotland*, ed. and tr. A. Constable, (Publications of the Scottish History Society, v. 10), Edinburgh 1892.

Manderston, William, *Tripartitum epithoma doctrinale et compendiosum in totius dyalectices artis principia Guillelmo Manderston Scoto nuperrime collectum*, Paris c. 1520 (in Bodl, NLS).

Manderston, William, *Bipartitum in morali philosophia*, Paris 1518 (in Bodl, GUL, NLS); Paris 1523 (in EUL); Paris 1528 (in ML, NLS).

Manderston, William, *Tractatus de futuro contingenti*, Paris 1523 (in BN).

Ockham, William, *Summa Logicae*, eds. P. Boehner, G. Gál, S. Brown, (Opera Philosophica 1), St Bonaventure, N.Y. 1974.

Richard de St Victor (Ricardus de Sancto Victore Scotus), in J.-P. Migne *Patrologia Latina*, Paris 1844–64 (221 vols.), vol. 196.

Richard de St Victor (Ricardus de Sancto Victore Scotus), *De Trinitate*, ed. J. Ribailler, in *Textes Philosophiques du Moyen Age*, 6, Paris 1958.

Tertullian, *Tertullian's Treatise on the Incarnation*, ed. and tr. Ernest Evans, London 1956.

Thomas Aquinas *see under* Aquinas, Thomas.

Waim, Gervasius, *Tractatus noticiarum*, Paris 1528 (in BL).

William Ockham *see under* Ockham, William.

SECONDARY LITERATURE

Adams, M. M., *William Ockham*, 2 vols, Notre Dame, Indiana 1987.

Barth, Karl, *Anselm: Fides quaerens intellectum: Anselm's proof of the existence of God in the context of his theological scheme*, London 1960.

Baudry, L., *La querelle des futurs contingents (Louvain, 1465–75)*, Paris 1950.

Beattie, W., 'Two notes on fifteenth century printing: I. Jacobus Ledelh', *Edinburgh Bibliographical Society Transactions*, vol. 3, 1950, pp. 75–7.

Boehner, P., *Collected Articles on Ockham*, ed. E. M. Buytaert, Louvain 1958.

Bonansea, B. M., O.F.M., 'Duns Scotus's voluntarism' in *John Duns Scotus 1265–1965*, eds J. K. Ryan and B. M. Bonansea, Washington, D.C. 1965.

Bonansea, B. M., O.F.M., *Man and his Approach to God in John Duns Scotus*, New York 1983.

Broadie, A., *George Lokert: Late-Scholastic Logician*, Edinburgh 1983.

Broadie, A., *The Circle of John Mair: Logic and Logicians in Pre-Reformation Scotland*, Oxford 1985.

Broadie, A., *Notion and Object: Aspects of Late-Medieval Epistemology*, Oxford 1989.

Broadie, A., *The Tradition of Scottish Philosophy*, Edinburgh 1990.

Broadie, A., *Introduction to Medieval Logic*, 2nd edn., Oxford 1993.

Broadie, A., 'James Liddell on concepts and signs' in *The Renaissance in Scotland*, eds M. Lynch, A. A. Macdonald, I. Cowan, Leiden 1994, pp. 82–94.

Brother Bonaventure *see under* Miner, Brother Bonaventure.

Bulloch, James, *Adam of Dryburgh*, London 1958.

Burns, J. H., 'John Ireland and "The Meroure of Wyssdome"', *Innes Review*, vol. 6, 1955, pp. 77–98.

Burns, J. H., '*Politia regalis et optima*: The political ideas of John Mair', *History of Political Thought*, vol. 2, 1981, pp. 31–61.

Burns, J. H., 'John Ireland: Theology and public affairs in the late fifteenth century', *Innes Review*, vol. 41, 1990, pp. 151–81.

Burrell, D., *Knowing the Unknowable God*, Notre Dame, Indiana 1986.

Copleston, F., *A History of Philosophy*, vol. 2, New York 1962.

Davie, G. E., *The Crisis of the Democratic Intellect*, Edinburgh 1986.

Davies, Brian, *The Thought of Thomas Aquinas*, Oxford 1992.

Dickinson, W. C. (ed.), *John Knox's History of the Reformation in Scotland*, London 1949.

Dunlop, Annie I., *Acta Facultatis Artium Universitatis Sancti Andree 1413–1588*, London and Edinburgh 1964.

Durkan, John, 'John Major: After 400 years', *Innes Review*, vol. 1, 1950, pp. 131–9.

Durkan, John, 'The school of John Major: Bibliography', *Innes Review*, vol. 1, 1950, pp. 140–57.

Durkan, John, 'The cultural background in sixteenth century Scotland', *Innes Review*, vol. 10, 1959, pp. 382–439.

Durkan, John and J. Kirk, *The University of Glasgow 1451–1577*, Glasgow 1977.

Élie, Hubert, 'Quelques maîtres de l'université de Paris vers l'an 1500', *Archives d'histoire doctrinale et littéraire du moyen âge*, vols. 25–6, 1950–1, pp. 193–243.

Farge, J. K., *Biographical Register of Paris Doctors of Theology 1500–1536*, Toronto 1980.

Frank, W. A., 'Duns Scotus on autonomous freedom and divine co-causality', *Medieval Philosophy and Theology*, vol. 2, 1992, pp. 142–64.

Geach, P. T., *God and the Soul*, London 1969.

Geach, P. T., *Providence and Evil*, Cambridge 1977.

Geach, P. T., *The Virtues*, Cambridge 1977.

Geach, P. T., 'Knowledge and belief in human testimony', in *The Past and the Present: Problems of Understanding: A Philosophical and Historical Enquiry*, Peter Geach, *et al.*, Oxford 1993, pp. 15–24.

Gilson, E., *The Christian Philosophy of St Thomas Aquinas*, London 1971.

Henninger, Mark G., S.J., *Relations: Medieval Theories 1250–1325*, Oxford 1989.

Hick, J. and A. C. McGill, *The Many-Faced Argument: Recent Studies on the Ontological Argument for the Existence of God*, London 1968.

John Paul II, 'The splendour of the truth shines'; encyclical letter *Veritatis splendor*, Libreria Editrice Vaticana 1993.

Kenny, A., 'Divine foreknowledge and human freedom', in *Aquinas: A Collection of Critical Essays*, ed. A. Kenny, London 1969, pp. 255–70.

Kenny, A., *The God of the Philosophers*, Oxford 1979.

Kenny, A., 'Form, existence and essence in Aquinas', in *The Heritage of Wisdom*, ed. A. Kenny, Oxford 1987, pp. 22–33.

Kenny, A., 'Philosophy of mind in the thirteenth century', in *The Heritage of Wisdom*, ed. A. Kenny, Oxford 1987, pp. 52–67.

Kenny, A., *Aquinas on Mind*, London 1993.

Kretzmann, N., A. Kenny, J. Pinborg (eds), *The Cambridge History of Later Medieval Philosophy*, Cambridge 1982.

Mackay, Aeneas J. G., 'Life of the author', in Mair's *A History of Greater Britain as well England as Scotland* (Publications of the Scottish History Society, v. 10), Edinburgh 1892.

Macken, R., 'La volonté humaine: faculté plus élevée que l'intelligence selon Henri de Gand', *Recherches de théologie ancienne et médiévale*, 42, 1975, pp. 5–51.

Macken, R., 'Les diverses applications de la distinction intentionelle chez Henri de Gand', in *Sprache und Erkenntnis im Mittelalter*, ed. J. P. Beckmann, *et al.*, Berlin and New York 1981.

Mackie, J. L., *Ethics: Inventing Right and Wrong*, Harmondsworth, Middlesex 1977.

Marenbon, John, *Later Medieval Philosophy (1150–1350): An Introduction*, London 1987.

Martin, C. F. J., 'The argument from authority', in *The Past and the Present: Problems of Understanding: A Philosophical and Historical Enquiry*, Peter Geach, *et al.*, Oxford 1993.

Mason, Roger A., 'Kingship, nobility and Anglo-Scottish Union: John Mair's *History of Greater Britain* (1521)', *Innes Review*, vol. 41, 1990, pp. 182–222.

Miner, Brother Bonaventure, 'The popular theology of John Ireland', *Innes Review,* vol. 13, 1962, pp. 130–46.

Moonan, Lawrence, *Lawrence of Lindores (d. 1437) on Life in the Living Being*, Ph.D. thesis, University of Louvain 1966.

Oberman, Heiko, *The Harvest of Medieval Theology: Gabriel Biel and Late-Medieval Nominalism*, Harvard 1967.

Ross, Anthony, 'Some Scottish Catholic historians', *Innes Review*, vol. 1, 1950, pp. 5–21.

Ryan, John K. and Bernardine M. Bonansea (eds), *John Duns Scotus, 1265–1965*, Washington, D.C. 1965.

Stolz, Anselm, 'Anselm's theology in the Proslogion' in *The Many-Faced Argument,* J. Hick and A. C. McGill, London 1968.

Swinburne, R., *Faith and Reason*, Oxford 1981.

Thorndyke, Lynn, *Michael Scot*, London 1965.

Torrance, T. F., 'La philosophie et la théologie de Jean Mair', *Archives de Philosophie*, vol. 32, 1969, pp. 531–47, and vol. 33, 1970, pp. 261–93.

Torrance, T. F., *The Hermeneutics of John Calvin*, Edinburgh 1988.

Villoslada, R. G., S.J., *La Universidad de Paris durante los estudios de Francisco de Vitoria, O.P.,* Rome 1938.

Wippel, John F., 'Aquinas's route to the real distinction: a note on *De ente et essentia*', *The Thomist*, 43, 1979, pp. 279–95.

Wippel, John F. and Allan B. Wolter, O.F.M., *Medieval Philosophy: From St Augustine to Nicholas of Cusa*, New York and London 1969.

Wolter, Allan B., O.F.M., 'Duns Scotus on the natural desire for the supernatural', *New Scholasticism*, vol. 23, 1949, pp. 281–317.

Wolter, Allan B., O.F.M., 'Duns Scotus, John', in *The Encyclopedia of Philosophy*, ed. Paul Edwards, New York 1965, vol. 2, pp. 427–36.

Wolter, Allan B., O.F.M., 'The formal distinction', in *John Duns Scotus, 1265–1965*, eds John K. Ryan and Bernardine M. Bonansea, Washington, D.C. 1965, pp. 45–60.

Wolter, Allan B., O.F.M., 'Native freedom of the will as a key to the ethics of Scotus', *Deus et Homo ad mentem I. Duns Scoti*, Acta Tertii Congressus Scotistici Internationalis Vindebonae, Sept. 28–Oct. 2, 1970, Rome 1972, pp. 359–70.

Wolter, Allan B., O.F.M., *The Philosophical Theology of John Duns Scotus*, ed. Marilyn McCord Adams, Ithaca 1991.

Index

Index

Hopkins, Gerard Manley, his 'Duns
   Scotus's Oxford' 7
Hugh of St Victor 2
human freedom *see* free will
humanism, development of 38

intellect
  and assent 19, 69, 80, 89, 91, 95
  and faith 12, 88–91, 97
  and values 20
  and vision 48, 49
  and will 11, 26–9, 32, 35, 41–50
    passim, 53–4, 56–7, 80, 86–7, 97
  knowledge located in 50
intellectualism
  and realism 20
  and universals 24–5
  and voluntarism 20, 24–5
  and will 42–4
Ireland, John 4, 21
  purpose of *Mirror of Wisdom* 55–6
  on divine grace 58
  on divine knowledge 59–62, 66–7,
    98
  on free will 56–7, 59, 98
  on hell 58–9

James IV 55
John Paul II 22

Kant, Immanuel 33 n. 2
Kenny, Anthony 16 n. 21
  on simultaneity of successive
    events 63, 68 n. 17
knowledge
  difference between faith and 72ff.
  divine *see* divine knowledge
  intellect the location of 57
Knox, John 5–6

Law of Nature 39–41
Lawrence of Lindores 4, 21
Liddell, James 4–5
Lokert, George 6, 62
  on assent of faith 80–1, 84 n. 13, 94,
    99 n. 9
  on assent to a proposition 70, 74, 77,
    83 n. 1, 83 n. 5
  on evident and inevident assent 79
  on highest evident assent 75

Lombard, Peter *see* Peter Lombard
love
  and will 35, 48, 57
  its primacy over knowledge 48,
    50, 57
Loyola, Ignatius 4

MacDiarmid, Hugh 5
Mackie, John L. 22
Mair, John 3, 5–6
  on evident assent 73, 83 n. 2
  on opinion 74
  on unity of the human mind 86
  on relation between will and
    faith 87–90
  on will and intellect 86, 89
Manderston, William 6, 62
Martin, C. F. J. 99 n. 7
Michael Scot 2
means–ends relations 50
mind,
  formalities of 28–9, 41, 45–6, 54, 86
  Henry of Ghent on powers of
    the 26–7
Monologion, Anselm's 10
motivum probabile 80–1, 91, 92
music, temporality of 65–6

natural will 30
negative freedom 30
Nihil volitum quin praecognitum 43, 48,
  49
nominalism 4
  and realism 20–1, 47
  and universals 24
  and values 23
  and voluntarism 20, 23, 47

Ockham, William *see* William Ockham
ontological argument, purpose of
  Anselm's 9–11
opinion
  distinction between evident assent
    and 79
  motivum probabile as rational basis
    of 80–1

Peter Lombard, his definition of
  faith 88
Plato 58

111